Sleeping With Spirit

A Journey with Psychic Dreams

Kim Treffinger

COPYRIGHT

Author photo on back cover by: Jennifer George

www.jennifergeorgephotography.com

Cover art and photography by: Kim Treffinger

Cover design by: Kim Treffinger

ACKNOWLEDGEMENTS

I would like to thank my family for their support in this project and allowing me to share some pieces of their life.

And I am deeply grateful to my friends who provided feedback on early drafts which closed some gaps for me, and particularly Karin H., and Chuck D. You helped me feel supported, which kept me on track and moving forward.

It is my hope that this book contributes to conversations about the nature of dreams and reality. Our dreaming life connects us to a vast stream of potential that is so untapped. The dream life is worthy of respect, even with all of the nonsensical dreams that happen. There is good there too, and it deserves more contemplation than Western culture currently gives it. These things will rarely be experienced if they are given little consideration.

I invite people to look into their dreams, and ask questions. Teach children to remember their dreams and record them

TABLE OF CONTENTS

INTRODUCTION

This is my story. Some names have been changed to preserve their privacy. There are many references to my former husband, and the choice to not use his name is intentional to honor his privacy as much as possible, and it just felt unnatural to use a fake name for my ex-husband. Some details have been combined for brevity, they have not been stretched or exaggerated. Integrity is paramount to me, and great care has been taken to write about my experiences honestly, and to the best of my memory.

The events shared are real. As real as anything is. It is my hope that readers take a look at their own dreaming life and discover unrealized potentials and spiritual connection, and embark on your own dream journey.

Part of my motivation for sharing this material is to spark more dialogue about dreams than is currently happening in Western culture. We sleep approximately 100 days a year, and roughly 20-25% of that is in REM sleep where vivid dreams and experiences usually occur. This amounts to about a month of every year that most people just throw away in terms of potential access to resources they give no consideration to. It is there waiting to be engaged and developed.

In our dreams we are travelers even more so than astronauts. We have access to this every time we close our eyes to sleep. We do not require a rocket ship to blast us into space. Without effort of a single muscle we can launch into the future, into the past, into other dimensions and spiritual realms from a very early age.

Dreams connect us with our natural spiritual self. Our connection can evolve over time when we decide to pay attention to it and take a look at what is offered there. To ignore this part of our life can slow down our spiritual growth.

It is my belief that everyone has the capacity to have psychic dreams, and make spiritual connections in their sleep. At what level this occurs depends on many things. I am writing this book because I hope that more people will give greater consideration to developing their dreaming life, and open themselves to the rich experiences that await. Experience another side of reality, spread the word and teach their children. It doesn't have to be something to fear. It is our natural way of being. And just because you might hear voices doesn't make you crazy.

Here I will share my early childhood and teen experiences that helped to form my acceptance of life after death and other dimensions of consciousness, and then I will share the very personal contents from dream journals kept consecutively and diligently over an eight year period highlighting psychic dreams and other spiritual events, and my experience of trying to make sense of them.

In the latter portion of the book I will discuss some dream fundamentals that I feel are a good base to have as a starting point, but keep in mind that I am not a scientist. I have studied a lot of psychology over the years after college where I was psychology major for over two years, but my intention is to give you an introduction, and hopefully increase your desire to go out and search for more information on your own.

Before I started writing this book I rarely discussed my dreams with people outside of my small group of friends and family. But after the dramatic experience that pushed me to start writing this book this year, I have talked with more and more people. My longtime friend Charles from high school told me he never remembered his dreams, and then went on to tell me about his father's dreams. While his father didn't write them down, he remembered them very well, and they were consecutive. They continued from where they left off the previous night. This had gone on for his whole life. I had never heard of that. A few days after our talk he had a precognitive dream about his brother in a helicopter crash. The discussion about dreams had made an impact on his consciousness. It was listening, and it responded.

I encourage anyone with similar experiences to venture out and read books that you feel called to, and write your own dreams down. You never know what you might find. This is possible for everyone.

"Our truest life is when we are in our dreams awake."
~ Henry David Thoreau

THE WAKE UP CALL

"Our life is composed greatly from dreams, from the unconscious, and they must be brought into connection with action. They must be woven together."~ Anais Nin

I have been a professional artist and photographer for over fifteen years. In 2001 I divorced after a long marriage to a Navy doctor who had been my college sweetheart, and I have been living alone with my pets in a nice middle class stucco house in the suburbs of San Diego, California, where I raised my son and daughter for the last nineteen years. My kids are now in their twenties and living in Los Angeles, happily creating their own lives. My son is an aspiring music producer and my daughter is in nursing school.

Art has been my life since I moved here.

In college, I had first dreamed of becoming a psychologist, partly to help me understand my father's mental illness, and partly because I wanted to help people. After 2 years of studying psychology, my path changed course when I hit a stumbling block related to a childhood trauma with math, and rather than seek help to overcome the issue, I decided to pursue design and art. Since 2005, I have been working as a professional photographer.

It was March, 2015.

My photographer girlfriend Rachel had been staying in my guest room a few nights a week since January, while she and her soon to be ex-husband were sorting out their legal details with custody of their three kids and support. And it was part of her escape from the drama there on her days off from her kids. She had gone up to LA for the weekend with a friend to shop for cameras. During lunch, they ran into the mother of a young teen medium named Tyler Henry.

Rachel tends to be one of those rare people who has things, people and opportunities come to her, and immediately, without thinking, will redirect it to the appropriate recipient. She called me up and said "I just met Tyler Henry's mother, you have to look him up." Tyler who? He does what? She said "he does psychic medium readings for celebrities, and he's only eighteen". Um, okay.

I didn't remember having any conversation with her that would lead her to connect me with the topic of a medium. She told me she knew I had been in touch with a few celebrities on Instagram, and it was the celebrity factor that she was connecting me with, not the mediumship per se. But to me, the mediumship element may as well have been a lit match to a fuse. It was no accident that this would be a prime "trigger for me", and I believe Rachel was guided to her connection with Tyler Henry's mother, just so she could share it with me and get this train moving.

I had met Rachel less than a year before, in the summer. We had both joined the same online professional portrait photography group. She messaged me when she saw that we lived near each other and she invited me to a model shoot she helped organize downtown in San Diego during the Comic Con. People were walking around in costumes. She had brought one of her regular male models, Ricardo, a handsome 26 year old Mexican and former Marine, guitar player.

We photographed him in the street next to a row of parked motorcycles, and in front of the passing train next to the convention center. He could charm any woman, and he was working it. With his guitar in hand, he looked like a rock star, and being Comic

Con, people thought he must be a celebrity, and came over to ask for his autograph and a photo with him. This was extremely amusing to us all, and we had a great time. Rachel and I had an instant connection.

It was like we were long lost sisters. We had a light-hearted competition to see who could get the better shots of Ricardo. She posted her favorite images online in black and white as she frequently did, and at that point in time it was really her "signature style" and what I associated her photography with.

Soon after, Rachel began to share her thoughts on separating from her husband Jack, and she asked me for advice on a variety of things relating to her rights during her divorce, and her photography business, and I became a sounding board for her on her daily dramas with her husband who was acting out in some malicious ways that were a great concern, including tracking her car and emails. So with her frequent stays at my house, there was some concern about whether he would be attempting to snoop on me as well.

This created a high level of tension, and contributed to our quick bonding. He told their middle daughter who I hadn't even met yet, that the divorce was my fault, which was just crazy and a flat out lie. This random, out of the blue, false accusation added an unexpected charge to our new connection.

Rachel is a gorgeous and lithe blue eyed woman with long black hair. She has three equally beautiful children with mesmerizing eyes. The eldest is a thirteen year old boy who is an actor, and he goes on casting calls and auditions in LA several times a week.

I found Tyler Henry's website, and there was not too much there that stood out to me. I scrolled to the bottom and noticed the name of his mentor psychic medium Lisa Williams. I found her book online and read her biography.

As I read, I started to have chills running up my spine, because her childhood sounded very similar to mine. I moved frequently, and had a terrible fear of going to sleep at night. I was convinced I heard footsteps going around my bed, no matter what house we were living in. I constantly called to my parents in the middle of the night to come check in the closet or under the bed. Just like her.

Reading her bio prompted me to think about my youngest brother James who had died in 1999 the day after Thanksgiving of an accidental alcohol and valium overdose when he was only twenty-seven years old. He was eleven years my junior. I wrote him a short note, as I sat at my computer to say I loved him, and I appreciated the dream I had about him a couple of months earlier.

In the dream I was outside on a lovely day by a tree lined residential street with some friends, and he rode up to me on a bicycle. I saw him off in the distance, but couldn't make out who it was at first. The bicyclist got closer and closer and in my mind I thought that couldn't be James? And sure enough it was. He stopped. I walked directly up to him and simply gave him a kiss on the mouth.

No words were spoken. It was just love. It was beautiful and felt so real. I felt the physical sensation of kissing him on the mouth. It was completely normal, but too quick and he was gone.

I realized later the bike was likely the one I had given him a few years before his death during a time of extreme hardship for him. The bike had been mine in college; a gift from my boyfriend (then future husband), and I wasn't ready to let go of the bike, but he needed it more than I did at the time. Unfortunately, it was stolen from him the next week, and it didn't provide the help I had hoped for after all. We both lost the bike. Seeing him on the bike gave me a sense of relief that he had the bike. It seemed he appreciated my desire to help him. And somehow it lessened my pain from not being able to help him more while he was alive. If there was ever anyone to go back in time and make a change for, he was it.

Well, the tears just started to flow, and I ended

up sobbing as hard as if he had just died yesterday, not sixteen years ago. I got up and wiped my tears, and went into the kitchen to my pack of four dogs who were behind the dog gate. I was still sniffling and wiping my eyes. All four dogs immediately raised the hair on their backs, they freaked out and started barking at me loudly as if a stranger had just walked into the room. I was the only one home with them.

I turned around and looked- what the heck? I felt a small pang of fear flash through me- is there someone else in the house? But there was nobody there. I did feel a denseness in the air behind my back, but I didn't see anything. The hair on my arms raised up and my scalp tingled, and I felt convinced it had to be James right there with me. I smiled and felt grateful for the experience. I thought, wow! That was a quick response!

I knew I had a large collection of spiritual books and journals packed in boxes in the garage where they had been for at least five years. I had amassed a collection of books during an intense period in my life of spiritual inquiry and experiences, and for a time I had been on a mission to prove there was more to life than my husband believed. I had tried to bridge a gap between us, but it only pushed us farther apart. My experiences were mystical and amazing at times.

They ranged from precognitive dreams, to seeing an apparition floating in the room in the middle of the night, which terrified me even though the image itself was not scary, to hearing a voice in my ear.

I would awaken and grab my husband's arm or try to climb over him to get out of bed and away from what I was seeing. After my marriage ended in 2001 I gave up on all of it. And when I thought I was going to have to sell my house, I packed up most of my personal belongings and kept them in the garage. When that period passed and I was able to stay, I never got around to unpacking the book boxes.

I decided to see if I could find a book in the garage that I knew I must have, by John Edwards, a psychic medium. I had read many spiritual books over the years on meditation, karma, psychic development, prophetic dreams, and many other areas of spiritual and personal growth. I pulled out all the books and found my journals. There were fourteen of them that I had recorded dreams between 1993 and 2001. Some of the pages had tabs on them from the last time I had reviewed them which must have been around 2002. The tabs marked the dreams that had come true and odd experiences.

Over a period of three days I reviewed over 2000 pages of the fourteen journals. I found many dreams that had come true, and some unusual experiences. I put more colored tabs on the "hits".

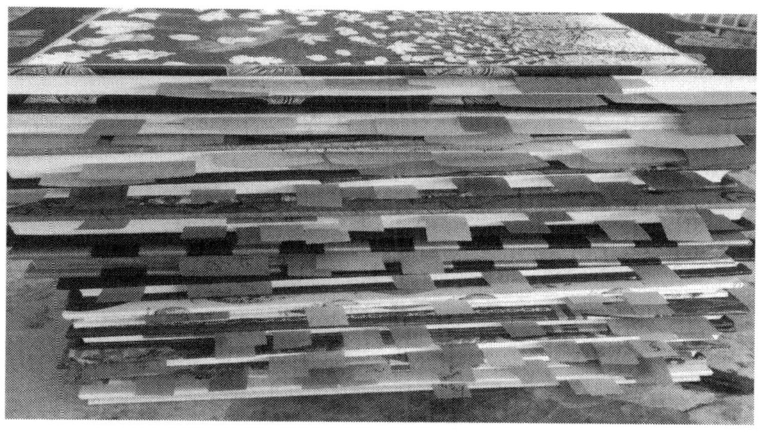

Stack of dream journals

It was very difficult to review the journals. It was like reliving that time of my life all over again. I was married to a Navy doctor, and we had two adorable little kids. I loved my husband very much, but our marriage was not a happy one.

I was a stay at home mom, and I was very depressed by the lack of connection with my husband. It was hard to be reminded of how much growing up I had to do back then. The most surprising thing was the discovery of dreams that came true ten to seventeen years after the dream. I would never have known without writing them, keeping the journals, and reviewing them again years later. One of the newly discovered dreams had the first name of a girlfriend in broadcasting ten years before I met her. She hired me many times to assist her on video shoots.

There was a 1997 dream of my next door neighbor Margaret driving a shiny new red Volkswagen Beetle. Her third child Emma was one year old. When Emma turned sixteen, she was given a shiny new red VW Beetle that now sits in front of my house every day while Emma is away at college.

Rachel came back from her trip to LA, and saw my kitchen counter piled with stacks of books from the garage that I wanted to reread, and all the journals I was reviewing. I also found two children's book stories I had written, and someday hoped to illustrate myself. I decided I was going to look into hiring an illustrator to do it for me so I could submit them to publishers. I had already done a preliminary search online and found some great artists I was excited about.

The next day Rachel called me on the phone to offer to illustrate a story for me. She said she had done illustration in college, and would love the chance to try. This was completely unexpected. I had no idea she had done illustration. I had not seen any of her artwork, and I had already fallen in love with illustrators I had seen, so I explained I was looking for an experienced artist.

I said I would love to see some of her art. With her upcoming divorce, impending move to a new home and three little kids to take care of in addition to running her own photography business, it didn't seem like something that was going to be a good fit right now anyway.

I was reviewing journal number twelve, and Rachel was packing some clothes in her room. On the first page of the journal was a dream entry from November 8th, 1997, that I had to read three times before I could speak any words. I realized that the dream was all about Rachel! Holy cow! Seriously? I was speechless. It was like a big joke of the universe had just been played on me. I hadn't even known Rachel for a year yet.

I called Rachel out from her room, and said you are not going to believe this! But you are in this journal from 1997! She laughed and said "What? You're giving me the willies!" I laughed too. It seemed crazy. Even for someone who had stacks of journals with dreams that had come true. I was blown away by this. Seventeen years ago? You can do that?! Wow.

In 1997 I would have still been married, and it had not even entered my head to become a portrait photographer. In fact, that idea did not occur to me until 2004, a little over 6 years later. I didn't even know anyone who was a photographer. The concept of being an independent portrait photographer had not even entered my head, as in I didn't know there was such a thing as a cottage industry in portrait photography. I thought you had to have a studio with lots of expensive equipment.

I read the entry to her.

"I was outdoors at a studio. Lots of metal buildings around. It seemed like there was an audition or casting call going on. I was sitting on a folding chair, and a woman younger than me with dark brown or black hair came up to me. She was a photographer and did black and white photos. She wanted to show me a photo that she did. It was a group of people behind a wooden gate.

It was young women behind it, their shoes showed under the bottom of the gate. I looked at it and I didn't know what to think about it, and how the shoes showed at the bottom. Somehow I didn't like that part of it. (There was a drawing I made of the gate with feet showing at the bottom). The girl who took the picture told me she was out of ink."

I showed Rachel the drawing in the journal, and asked her if she had ever photographed anyone behind a gate like that, and she said no. Just the day before she had offered to illustrate my children's book, but she hadn't done any illustrations since college. She was not *out* of ink, she was not *in* her ink. At this point I didn't understand the gate portion of the dream, and was ready to brush it off as something that just didn't fit, but I was so excited about the other relevant things: female photographer younger than me (five years) with dark brown/black hair, who did black and white photography, with auditions and casting calls (her son is an actor who is frequently doing auditions and casting calls- interestingly he was not even BORN at the time of the dream!- I will discuss this aspect later).

A few days later she invited me to a real estate shoot she was doing for a four million dollar home in La Jolla that was recently remodeled.

There had been young female models there earlier who she photographed all around the house. She took me on a tour of the home and we went upstairs to the master bedroom. There was a balcony outside to the front of the house with a very nice decorative white railing with a familiar crossbar pattern. As I stood there, absorbing the design of the railing, it dawned on me that it was very similar to the gate in my drawing, Rachel was busy taking photos inside the master bedroom.

She was at the fireplace that had a glass door on it, and she was complaining that she was having trouble getting a good shot of it. She said "**I don't like how my feet are showing up at the bottom!**" I got chills again, and laughed out loud. I said Oh my God! You just finished that dream! She said "stop giving me the willies!"

I could not believe it! The dream had finished right in front of us. That was about as big of an A-ha! Moment as I can ever remember. I took a photo of the railing on my phone, and a photo of the drawing in my journal, and sent it out to several friends and family.

The synchronicity required to line all of this up is beyond my ability to comprehend.

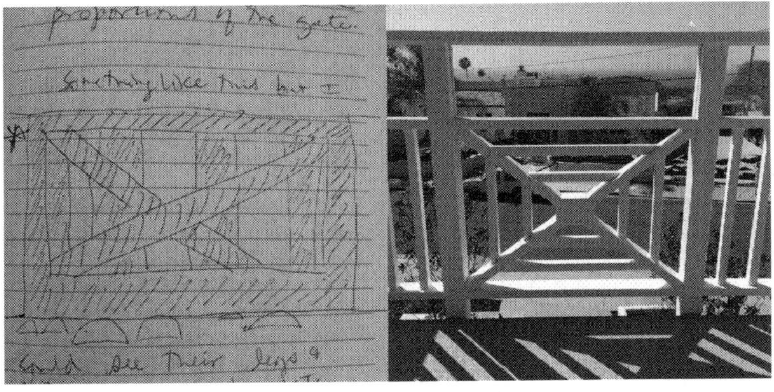

Clearly it is not an identical match in the drawing, but combined with the other elements in the dream it ties together very strongly. And it was seventeen years earlier!

It was as if the dream was a seed planted in 1997, waiting to be discovered and completed seventeen years later, at a time when it could play out with a witness, and give me the impetus to write this book. I had stopped recording my dreams in 2001. I had to be nudged to get those books out and review in time to find the gate that would match the event. There had to be something in there that would be discovered later when I was brought back to looking into all of this again, or I might never have done anything with them. And I see now, that would have been a waste of all the dedication I put into keeping the journals for eight years. And here it had been hiding in a box in my garage for years!

I pulled out a separate journal I had kept, of synchronicities that still had a lot of empty pages, and decided to resume my dream journaling. I wrote down at the top March 13, 2015, "Ready to resume" Then I flipped to the front to see what I had written there years ago, and I saw the last entry was dated March 13, 2006. I was starting again nine years later to the day! Something was telling me I was right on time. Who needs a clock? I laughed out loud.

I knew it was time to write this book. And while I have been working on it, new discoveries have presented themselves. I have an overwhelming sense that more realized dreams are waiting to be found. I resumed keeping a dream journal, and right away new things began to happen.

ABOUT THE DREAM WORLD

From what I have seen, most researchers studying dreams in a college setting disregard any spiritual involvement in dreams. The assumption primarily being that it would likely not be accepted by the college as at least one reason to cast it aside. But dreams are part of our spiritual core, and to ignore this, is to only look at a very small portion of what dreams are about. They are using the wrong methods and everything they think they see is colored by their assumption that the soul does not exist in dreams. And then they complain that people do not want to take part in their groups. It doesn't surprise me.

When we sleep, whether it's day time or night time, our astral body or energy body leaves our physical body for a short time, (though it remains attached, so it is instantly able to find its way back) and travels in the spirit world. In the spirit world things in the past, present, or future may be happening simultaneously.

Our dreaming mind may dream in a few categories. There may be more than I am aware of presently, but basically people will find their dreams fall into these categories: Processing, Planning, Psychic, Lucid or Spiritual (spiritual does not mean religious here).

Psychic dreams can be about any time, past, present or future. They can be of the same day, sometime in the past or many years in the future. They can be other possible potentials that we may or may not choose to bring into being.

This ties together with the idea that our thoughts create our reality. Including our sleeping thoughts if we give enough concentration and power to them. When these events include other people, it is because on a telepathic level they have agreed to bring it into being. Many agreements are already underway in developing the manifestations of what we want to have in our life.

The dreamer may experience the fluid nature of the spirit world, in terms of people or surroundings, and events changing with little or no warning. One story can blend into another, and many times parts of two or more stories can be happening in the same dream.

You may experience yourself in someone else's shoes quite literally, and think that what you are seeing is about yourself, when in reality it is someone else or someone close to you. This becomes evident when the story makes more sense by placing the other person in the role that you thought you were playing, and it can be temporary for just part of the story and then by switching you back into that character again the story works out. Unfortunately, at first glance the dream will likely seem to make no sense to you, until it plays out at some point in time, possibly even many years in the future.

There may be many confusing elements, which make deciphering dreams a challenge at times. One dream might be completely straight forward, including an exotic name or a specific quote that someone later says, and others might be foggier and even abstract. A radio signal is a good analogy.

Sometimes you have great reception, and other times there is a lot of static. At times you may go to another level and the information you get is very abstract with geometric symbols and ancient images that seemingly make no sense. That doesn't mean the information is not valid, it's just harder to make out what it is saying.

There are things we can do to improve our radio signal. And then sometimes our dreams are just playing out a mash up of internal emotions and processing unrealized desires, regrets and whatever struggles we may be going through in our waking life or having some play time. We dream about what interests us in one way or another, or what we have some level of connection to.

Our consciousness is divided into two areas. Waking and sleeping time. But they can overlap. Our higher consciousness that interacts on a spiritual level is with us even when we are awake, and it is what we might call our "still small voice", our "hunch" or "gut feeling" and intuition. It is that part of us that is timeless, while obviously, our physical body has a limited lifespan.

How many of us give little thought to our sleeping life at all. We just let it happen. Quality of sleep is our biggest concern. How many hours of sleep we got last night. Can we sleep in?

But what if I told you that your sleeping life is as vibrant as your waking life, that your energy body is often times going on great adventures, and traveling to the future, if only you were capturing it all first thing in the morning before it was lost. **Just imagine**. How many times I have heard people just brush it off, as if it doesn't apply to them. If you are *human* it applies to you.

When I began keeping dream journals in 1993 I never imagined it would develop into eight years of dedicated dream journaling with 14 journals, averaging 160 pages each, dozens of dreams that would come true and a wide variety of mystical and spiritual experiences and synchronicities. I had almost forgotten that I actually started recording my dreams when I was a teenager, and my first psychic dream was recorded in 1976 when I was 14.

Dreams of disasters, crossed over loved ones, other living family members, future friends, past and future relationships, pets, celebrities, and even a President, have made the review process a treasure hunt of sorts. Pages and pages and pages of dreams that **don't click** to go through, and BAM! Something pops up and I knew I had read through that journal at least two times before, and somehow I missed it when I read about my son's dog that he would "randomly" decide to get and bring home without even asking when he was a freshman in college and still living at home, and the dream was only THIRTEEN years before! Because I hadn't figured out how to decipher it yet- not until I read it three times. And then it made so much sense. Because I *was my son in the dream,* though I looked like myself to me, so that when I wrote the dream in the journal thirteen years before, I thought it was all about me.

Well it was largely ABOUT me with the back story, but when I placed my son in my place in the dream, all the pieces fit together perfectly.

So this is not about trying to stretch the truth, the majority of my recorded dreams did NOT come true. This is about looking at dreams in a more spiritual and ethereal way. Many things can be different than they are in waking life, they may have an obvious reason or it may not yet be known to us.

Part of the dream may happen at another time entirely. You may be shown an event that will happen, but the people involved are not revealed by the faces of the people you know, so that when it happens three days later, you are surprised by the event itself, and not the fact that you had already dreamt about it, which you won't discover until you do your journal pages review the following week.

The spirit world is a very fluid place. Things and people and events can be multi-dimensional, multi layered and just really amazing. It can make you feel like you are a detective on the biggest story of your life, or even of all of humanity if you really want to know.

Of the well over 2500 pages of dream journals and daily pages that were kept, the vast majority of dreams that were logged, appear to be little more than processing a fantasy life and replaying petty bits of emotional experience and reminding myself I have a lot more to learn. A very humbling experience in itself reviewing that kind of content. I would think "note to self", put in a request for no more celebrity dreams. You will begin to see a pattern. And you might ask why bother writing it down? And that is a good question. Partly I think, to allow yourself to see that you are reaching for more, you are experiencing a variety of levels of clarity or confusion. And later you will see that your dreams are evolving. The more you begin to analyze them and give them more space in your life, you will be rewarded to see how they change.

Why would you bother to write down a dream you had of being locked in a room with a giant anaconda who was going to try to swallow you whole? If you are like me, and you don't remember your dreams for more than ten minutes after waking, you would miss out potentially on a "mini" hit when your son requests a brand new book that arrived in the mail that day at bedtime, and when you turn to the page with an Anaconda on it, and your son points to it and says "can a snake like that swallow you whole?", you might miss the experience of "holy cow!"

The dream was full of drama, and the way it played out was rather entertaining to someone who was new at this at the time. It's good to have those little "gem" moments that keep you going. You just never know when something is going to pop up. They are a small way to show you that your connection is working.

Now, other than illustrating how you can get a "hit", is that kind of dream going to help someone in their life? Probably not, but just like children's books teach us step by step, I think these kind of mini hits are like bait to get us to pay attention and look for more. I also see that the analogy of a children's book here, for me, even learning about the stage that I was at back then, really was like experiencing these things from a childlike perspective. And these little tidbits that involved my kids were an easy way to share what was happening to me with them, and bringing them into my experience with children's book subject matter.

This was an opportunity to talk with my children about other kinds of connections we can have with people. In those days I was on the fence about how much of this to share with my children because I knew my husband didn't believe any of it. I didn't particularly want to put my kids in the middle, and yet by not sharing it more deeply with them, they were still in the middle in terms of now they were in a more vague space, and it was just something that wasn't deeply discussed because I didn't want to rock the boat more than I already had.

It is that looking for more that keeps us going. When you start to make connections in the dream realm and see them play out in various ways in your waking life, you will start to wonder what else is possible.

I am not here to share the muck of the dreams that did not happen, or even the big spiritual messages of predictions of future disasters, even though I have had a few of those, floods, fire, earthquakes, many other people have already made similar predictions and that is not my focus.

As far as I can tell, the dreams that have come true were seemingly random, and no effort on my part was required during sleep. They seem in some ways to be a gift, and yet I believe it is a result of going to sleep with the "radio turned on". Not an actual radio, but being open to receive.

What I do hope to bring about is an increased interest in the dreaming life of humanity. There is much we can learn from it, and so many things to do, whether it be get help finding answers or guidance on personal matters, or whether you have an interest in spiritual growth and you would like to connect with your guides and master teachers, and even God. All of these things and more can be achieved with these three things: Attention, Intention and Practice.

Remember that we sleep more than 50 hours a week, 200 hours a month, roughly 100 days out of the year we are asleep! One third of our life! We are dreaming and having amazing experiences that can teach us many things, and yet dreams are brushed off by the majority of people as something that is hardly worth any consideration. I repeatedly see people scrunch their eyebrows and express a confused look on their face as they struggle to imagine why in the world anyone would take a dream seriously.

Dreams connect us to our spiritual core. If someone has a desire to grow spiritually, and experience more than just waking physical reality, getting involved with your dreaming life, along with meditation is going to have great beneficial potential.

Attention involves a conscious effort to be present for your dreaming life. Develop a desire to experience more, and to engage with it mentally on a daily basis. Imagine yourself remembering your dreams and recording them for review at a later time.

Imagine yourself planning to request assistance from your dreams with issues in your waking life.

Intention. Decide to give your dream time a higher priority in your life. Gradually increase the priority as you develop your engagement with it. When your dreams begin to acknowledge your attention, and present you with more interesting dream content, increase your attention to working with your dreams.

Practice. Keep a dream journal and pen (or other recording device or materials) by your bed at all times. Become diligent in recording as much of your dream memory as you can, immediately upon waking. Dreams are frequently like a misty fog that evaporates as our waking self comes to more alertness into the physical world, and thoughts of starting our day begin to take over. The dream will float away into the background.

If you can only remember one sentence at first, write it down! Gradually there will be more and more. If you cannot remember anything, try writing three pages of anything at all to empty your mind a little bit. A brain dump to make room for more and also tell your higher self that you are serious about wanting to remember your dreams, and this will help you to program that desire, and it will develop.

We dream for a reason. At the very least, you will see that there is much more to life than just our physical waking reality. Many people have written books on a variety of levels of dreams and related topics. This is not really new information, but it is my hope that the experiences presented here will speak to the people who need to hear this.

For the skeptics, there are people who have made up their minds that they already know everything they need to know. Their belief system either follows strict biblical or religious texts, or what is currently known by physical science. I do not expect everyone to believe this, but there are enough studies and stories at the present time to prove there is more to life than current science can explain completely.

Many skeptics that I have encountered believe things are only allowed to be confirmed as real or valid if they follow rules of the physical world. A non-linear dream with multiple layers and partial information would likely be brushed off by a skeptic. You can't measure the energy or dream world the same way as you can the physical world.

You will not find these type of experiences as commonly accepted. A quick search online for information about dreams from scientific studies seems to be completely devoid of any mention of psychic or spiritual experiences with dreams, and generally brush them off as "hypnogogic hallucinations". Yet there has been a recent discovery by a psychologist (Dr. Allan Botkin) treating former soldiers suffering from PTSD, that inducing a REM state while awake, has been able to connect the patient with the dead person who is the source of their grief, and experience permanent relief as a result of the encounter where they saw the person whole and happy and forgiving in the non-physical world.

Dr. Botkin reports that some of the sessions were in fact witnessed by an assistant who experienced the same thing as the patient. With over 20 years of practicing this technique on thousands of patients, this technique is now being taught to thousands of licensed therapists around the world today.

As long as someone is in resistance to the possibility of other levels of reality, they are not going to experience it. A big part of all of this is that it is largely a permission based experience. But I will say, then what is the harm in deciding to hold an open mind for a period of time and check it out. Without an open mind, there will likely be no experience. They can't know what they don't know. They need to look at this side of life with new eyes.

I have been honest about the experiences here, provided dates of the dream and date of the event that followed in most cases. If I wanted to make anything up, I'm sure I could have come up with better stories than some of the ones I have shared here. And if I was trying to get famous off of predicting presidential mishaps, why in the world would I wait twenty years to share them?

I lived with a skeptic for many years and I know the feeling of being ostracized for believing my experiences were real. In time they will learn there is more than they had been willing to see. Everyone has their own time for their path to evolve.

SPIRITED FAMILY

"Go confidently in the direction of your dreams! Live the life you've imagined. As you simplify your life, the laws of the universe will be simpler". ~ Thoreau.

Like everyone, my experiences and ideas about death were informed by my childhood experiences and family stories that were shared with me. When I was little, I spent a lot of time with my mother's parents while my mother was at work. My maternal grandmother Mary was one of 11 children in Wilkes-Barre, Pennsylvania. Born in 1913, she was the fourth eldest. Her father worked in the coal mines and her mother did her best to keep the kids in line, but she was often sick with kidney disease and confined to bed. As a teenager, my grandmother was expected to carry on with the chores and watch after the younger ones.

The youngest was Leo who was slightly crippled from Polio. Her younger sister Ruth was nine when my grandmother sent her to the store to buy candy for Leo. Ruth was hit by a car on her way home. Word got to my grandmother who rushed to her, picked her up and carried her on foot, to a nearby doctor's office. Upon entering the office with her dying sister, she was told to leave, for fear it might frighten patients who were waiting. Her sister Ruth died in her arms.

My grandmother was traumatized by the loss of her favorite sister, and felt responsible because she had sent her to the store. She would later name her first daughter after Ruth. Shortly after that, her mother died from kidney failure.

My grandmother was downstairs in the kitchen with her other sisters when she saw her dead mother coming down the stairs. She saw her mouth open and close to speak, but no words came out. In shock, my grandmother ran outside to the backyard. For years, she wished she had stayed there to hear the message her mother was trying to bring her. There was a degree of acceptance in life after death as a result.

When I was three, my family was living in San Bruno, California. My dad Philip was 24 and my mom

Judie was 22. My little brother Philip was about 14 months old. My father was suddenly stricken with severe schizophrenia that manifested rather violently out of the blue, and I witnessed him knocking my mother unconscious with a wine bottle in front of me and my little brother. I saw her lying unconscious on the floor in front of me. But I don't remember any sounds or emotion attached to the event. It has remained one of my first memories in life.

We had to move away from my dad after that, and then, we had infrequent visits. So I never got to really know the man my dad was before his illness set in. A few months later, my mother was driving home from a night out for her birthday and she fell asleep at the wheel and crashed her car. The paramedics arrived, and found her unconscious, not breathing and covered in blood. Not finding a pulse, they assumed she was dead. They made no effort at CPR, and put her in the back of the ambulance and covered her with a sheet. My mother remembers watching all of this, and seeing her body covered up, while standing beside her on the side of the road, was her maternal grandfather who had died when I was a baby. He had been a huge support to her during and after her accidental teen pregnancy with me. She was happy to see him and very confused about what she was looking at.

Her Grandpa told her "you are going to be ok", "you have to go back". And with that she was back in her body, coughing up blood. The paramedics heard her coughing and started to freak out. She's alive! She was taken to the hospital, received stitches under her nose, and was sent home the same day. It was clearly a miracle that she survived her birthday, despite the lack of action by the paramedics.

A couple of years later, my mother started dating a tall handsome Navy man who looked a bit like Steve McQueen. In fact people mistook him many times for the actor. And they decided to get married when I was five. There was an engagement party at a clubhouse pool. I remember being told to take a walk down a grassy slope toward some train tracks with my dad and my soon to be new dad. I had no idea I was the topic of discussion, as my natural dad was essentially handing me over to my new dad.

My dad's illness made it impossible to have much contact with him since his connection to reality came and went so quickly. My new dad agreed to adopt me and my younger brother, and I would not see my birth father again until I was nineteen.

One night after the wedding, when everyone was asleep, my mother went downstairs to the living room and saw her dead grandfather sitting on the couch. He wanted to toast her new marriage. There were two glasses on the coffee table and they clinked glasses and he wished her well. In the morning she thought it must have been a dream, but when she went downstairs there were two wine glasses on the table with water in them, and my dad asked her where she went during the night.

She knew it had felt totally real, one of the most real experiences she had ever had. She had been very close to her grandfather, so close that she called him Father just as her mother did, and her own father she called Daddy. He had been particularly supportive to her during her accidental teen pregnancy with me, which was a taboo in the early 60s, and a great embarrassment to my grandmother who shamed my mom. So her grandfather was a great ally for her prior to his death.

We soon moved to Lomita California for my third school for kindergarten, and the start of first grade. My dad was going on deployment soon, and one night we had been out to pick up dinner. When we arrived home, our apartment door was wide open. We all stood at the door afraid to go inside in case there was a burglar still inside. Within seconds, a police officer arrived.

We assumed that a neighbor had reported the break in. But the officer was there for another reason.

My dad's mother had committed suicide that day in a complicated and dramatic plot that involved putting her car on a hill at the cemetery, and allowing it to run her over after she had taken an overdose of pills, and she had failed at trying to gas herself inside her car with a hose and exhaust fumes. Well it was incredibly shocking and horrible news, but it didn't explain why our door was wide open. My dad went inside to check and there was nobody there. Whatever devastation he must have felt over his mother's suicide, he kept from us.

My adoptive dad's father had died when my dad was a baby, in a car crash. His mother was the driver and his father the passenger. I believe she was possibly never the same again after that trauma. I had only met her a few times. I didn't find out until recently, that she had opposed my parents' marriage. She had not approved of his decision to marry a woman with two children.

Just the week before she took her life, she tried to make amends and she paid us a visit and brought presents for my brother and myself. After her death, unusual things started happening in the apartment immediately. Kitchen cupboard doors opened and closed. Lights would flicker, wind would come through our apartment with all the windows closed. Our puppy Lamb Chop seemed to be getting kicked by some invisible force. My dad made jokes about the Boogie man hiding in the closet in the living room, and then he went out to sea for months. While he was gone, my mother's parents came to visit, partly because we didn't like these odd things happening.

It was a two bedroom apartment. My Grandmother slept with my mom and my Papa slept with my brother and I in our room. In the middle of the night we all woke up to someone screaming very loudly. My Papa jolted out of bed and ran to my mother's room. It was my mom and Grandma screaming like little girls! I wasn't told until many years later, but they woke up to see a black fog in their room, and all three of them saw it, and they felt it was pure evil whatever it was. But it vanished and was never seen again. What do I make of it? I'm not totally sure, but I doubt it was pure evil. That doesn't mean it wasn't scary, as I'm sure it was. Was it the sad and confused soul of my dad's mother? What it something else?

It could have been a spirit connected to the apartments where we were living, and the dynamic between my mother and her mother attracted it, or maybe it was a manifestation of their own future emotional turmoil together that would play out dramatically many years later, when during an argument they both lost their senses and got into a wrestling match trying to do bodily injury to each other. Personally, I think it was the latter. They were being given a chance to be in fear of something together, which could have brought forth more bonding, and healing past wounds which was needed.

By second grade we had moved to Manhattan Beach, California, right across the street from the beach. It was a kid's dream. I loved my teacher, and found an immediate crush with a boy named Todd, and a couple of really wonderful girlfriends.

We spent many days in the spring and summer down on the sand learning to do handstands and cartwheels, and boogie boarding in the waves. Some of my happiest childhood memories happened there. Our house was divided into apartments. We had the downstairs unit. We had a dog and three cats. One day I was in the living room, and I noticed a specific smell that I had somehow always associated with the old smell of my pacifier from when I was a baby. I was aware that the smell was familiar, and that it had probably been around me even long after I gave up my pacifier.

This set some confusion in my mind, and being almost eight years old, I was able to formulate a question about it and called out to my mom in the kitchen. "Mom what's this smell that is following me?" She came over from the kitchen and said "what are you talking about?" and she sniffed the air around me and down closer to where I was standing. Her eyes got really big, her body sort of leaned back with surprise and she immediately said "that's the smell my grandfather had on him when he was in the hospital dying of cancer". Oh. Ok.

So there was a brief explanation, that his spirit must be with us, and "he is probably looking out for you". "Like a ghost?" I asked, "I guess so". She loved her grandfather a lot, so it was an emotional event for her. I don't think she had told me much about him until that point. And she was surprised that he was following me around or at least hanging out with us.

At the same time all of this is happening, my Catholic raised mother enrolled my brother and I in Catechism school. We went to a lovely Black woman's house to learn about Jesus, and forgiveness, and sin and church, and confession. She played piano for us and we learned songs about Jesus. First communion was a special event and I got a fancy white dress, and my best friend Laura was going to the same first communion with me. When I had to go do a confession in a private booth with a priest, it was a very odd experience. I was a really good kid and I couldn't think of anything to confess, so I actually made something up! How ironic. I lied in confession because I didn't have anything to confess.

HAWAIIAN LIFE

For third grade we moved to Pearl City on the island of Oahu, Hawaii. When we first arrived, there was no housing available for us, so we stayed in a hotel room in downtown Honolulu.

A flock of pigeons flew into our room every day looking for bread crumbs, which just delighted my brother and me. We learned that there was going to be a Hawaiian parade that weekend, and in the alley behind the hotel there were several floats being assembled. We hung out long enough to get invited to help stick flowers on a float.

Our parents had no idea what we were up to, but it was so much fun. Then housing opened up, and we moved on base into a townhome near a sports field that was peppered with mango trees that we learned how to climb. During little league season we would climb the mango trees and pick them to eat, like apples. The really soft ripe ones got picked for mango fights and we threw them at each other. They practically exploded and we were covered in mango mush.

Back at the end of the field was an area close to Pearl Harbor. Ruins from the war that had once been buildings. We would go exploring in this one remnant of a building right on the water and there was evidence of what had once been a kitchen. There was also a dock nearby and we would go out on the dock and look at fish swimming in the water. One day my brother fell in and people were in a panic to get him out because there were hammer head sharks in the water. Thankfully he was unscathed, but it was pretty scary all the same.

My mother put me in a hula class and we wore fake grass skirts. I thought I was getting pretty good. There were also plumeria bushes everywhere. A friend of mine and I went around with a paper bag picking plumerias, and when the bag was full we went home and with a needle and thread strung them together into leis, and kept them in the refrigerator.

On Fridays we went door to door with our leis selling them for $1 each. Sometimes I would come home with $10. For a nine year old that was pretty good! I loved how the flowers smelled. I soaked in all the Hawaiian smells, the red dirt, stinky monkey pod trees, the banana tree we had in our back yard. I think I was bombarded with smells there, and this was probably where I began to develop my strong sense of smell.

The bedrooms in our townhouse were all upstairs. I had my own room and my brother's room was across the hall from mine. I had difficulty sleeping and frequently would be frightened in the middle of the night by the sound of creaky stairs, as if someone was coming up the stairs. It was a chronic problem. A hall light had to be on, or a night light in my room. And inevitably a call out to my mom or dad to come check my room because I heard something.

One night I was particularly certain that someone was coming to take me away. I heard footsteps on the stairs. My parents were in bed. This night, rather than call them, I went and got in bed with my brother. Still, I heard the footsteps coming. I told my brother to get under the bed with me. I decided we were going to outsmart whoever was coming for me. I remember us going under the bed. I heard the steps get closer to the hall way and enter the room. Footsteps came over to my side of the bed and I saw black pants and pointed black men's boots standing next to the bed. He stood there for a few moments and then turned and left.

In the morning, my brother and I were back in bed. I asked him about the man who came in the room and he didn't know what to say to me. I immediately told my parents. They sat my brother and I on the couch and questioned us. They were very concerned that someone may have broken into the house.

No doors or windows were unlocked. I realized that my brother's bed was so low to the ground that physically we would not have been able to get our heads under the bed- so how did we do it? Did we do it? What really happened? It was so real! It was definitely a mystery that I wondered about for years. Now I think it was an out of body experience we had, and some spirit being was coming to check on us.

In Fourth grade we bought a red Volkswagen camper van and moved to Haleiwa on the North Shore. We were in a little house on the highway in the middle of nowhere but next to a sugar plantation that gave us a jungle in the backyard. There was a Japanese candy store in walking distance on the way to school that we would stop at sometimes for chocolate and the owners were usually in the back where they lived with their family, so we learned to call out "Mama-san!" and the shopkeeper would come to the counter to help us.

Sometimes we got rice candy with a rice paper wrapper that would dissolve in our mouth. My mother's parents came to visit and we drove them around the whole island in our van in one day sightseeing.

We had new pets at this house, and my cat Pookie a white cat with grey patches of stripes was not spayed and she got pregnant from a stray out back. Pookie was my life. She slept with me every night.

We didn't have television at this house and we had to make our own amusements. We would play my mother's old records on my record player I had gotten for my eighth birthday and I would sing along and dance in my room by myself.

Sometimes my brother and I would make up silly games. We invented a goofy game where we took turns piling pillows and blankets on top of each other into a tower and then the one outside of the pillows would run and take a big jump onto the one under the pillows.

We imagined the pillows were an igloo, and we called it Eskimo Babies. How two little kids living in the jungle in Hawaii could associate pillows with igloos and Eskimos I don't really know. But we didn't have air conditioning either, so maybe we were just trying to imagine a cooler place. We both took turns jumping on the other, and lucky for us that nobody got hurt.

Well one night Pookie crawled under my sheets as she frequently did to sleep with me. I woke up in the middle of the night a soaking mess. I had no idea why. Then I felt some tiny things moving at the foot of my bed near my feet and I took a peek down there and I saw Pookie and two little baby kittens! I jumped out of bed and ran to tell my mom and dad… Pookie is having her babies!! And they are in my bed!! I was so excited. I had no idea what to do. It was better than any Christmas gift I could possibly imagine.

My mom grabbed her laundry basket and put a towel in it, and then moved Pookie and the two babies into the basket in my room. She had me change my pajamas and get cleaned up. She changed the sheets on my bed and everyone went back to bed. In the morning there were two more babies with Pookie. She had four babies!

I was beside myself with excitement, and joy and love. I had never felt so much love for anything in my life. I named all of the babies immediately. Kama, Love, Rudolph and Junior (Junior looked just like Pookie). Over the next few weeks I would be mesmerized watching them nurse, and what a good mom Pookie was carrying them from one place to another in my room.

I was so happy, that I even imagined the tree outside my bedroom window to be my friend and that it would dance with me as it fluttered in the wind while I was inside my room. A friend of my mother who visited occasionally told her that my aura was all gold. I had no idea what that meant. But he believed it meant I had pure energy. This was the first time I had ever heard of energy for people.

I came home from school one day and the cats were not there. I asked my mom where they were. She told me they had gotten sick and were throwing up, and she took them to the vet and they all had heart worm, and had to be put to sleep.

I was in shock. I was devastated. I had a million questions. How did I not see that they were sick? Why did they have to be put to sleep? It just didn't make any sense. I went around the room and I collected bits of their hair and I put it into a little keepsake box and I cried myself to sleep at night. It was possibly more than I could bear. I grieved Pookie and her babies for a solid year.

Many years later after I had children of my own, my dad confided that the cats did not have heartworm, but they had learned my brother had asthma as a result of being allergic to cats and they were afraid I would blame my brother, and that I wouldn't understand why the cats had to go. They were wrong. Disappointment over the truth would have been much less painful than being told they all died. I had an intense understanding of the value of the truth after this. Even though I wasn't told the truth as a child, deep down I knew something didn't add up. It was only validated years later.

Fifth grade came, and I had new teachers. I read books like crazy and my primary teacher Mr. Ball had reading contests all the time. It was always a close race between my friend Patty and I to see who could read the most books.

The winner would get interesting prizes, like an antique Hawaiian soda bottle from his collection, or the chance to conduct the Christmas Choir. I wanted to direct the choir very badly. I read every Nancy Drew book, The Hardy Boys, I read veterinary books on diseases of cows that my dad had on a shelf from one of his college classes. After losing the kittens I was seriously thinking about becoming a veterinarian, to prevent that from happening again and help save other animals.

One night we were all at the kitchen table while my brother and I were doing our homework. It was dark outside, and we heard a car go by fast, screeching tires, a loud thump and yelp. There were no street lights since we were kind of in the middle of nowhere. My parents did not go look out front to see what it was.

My brother and I rode the bus to school every day and the stop was right out in front of our house. At the place where we had to stand to wait for the bus was a big hairy dead dog. It seemed like a Golden Retriever. It was very sad seeing it lying there while we waited for the bus. Day after day the bus would come while we waited next to the dead dog.

Flies began to swarm around it, the smell of death seeped out, and the body began to rot away. It was a pretty awful sight for anyone. And somehow, not the bus driver who saw us standing there every day next to this decomposing dog, or either of my parents had a thought to call animal control to pick it up, or even to try to bury it themselves.

And as I waited there for the bus, I could only imagine the life it must have had, where was it going? Did the owners miss him? Well obviously they didn't take very good care of him if he wandered off and got killed.

I created little stories in my mind about what he had done in his life, and how he felt about now becoming a pile of bones on the street in front of my house. It was very odd. I always felt very sad for him as I stood there.

I knew what loss was after having lost all my kittens and their mother the previous year. Life could be very tough for animals, and for kids who cared about them.

I thought more and more about becoming a veterinarian. And one day the bus stop dog was just bones and some wisps of fur. Almost as if he had never been there at all.

My mother had a baby boy and the never ending circle of life continued. When she was pregnant again almost immediately, it was time to move back to the mainland.

My Grandparents were concerned if we stayed there much longer, my brother and I would not be able to speak proper English anymore. We were already wise to all the pigeon English our barefooted classmates and friends used. "You like da kine?" (meaning – do you want some?)

And I needed more help with math after my racist Filipino math teacher made fun of me in class and said "Stupid **Haoli** girl (slang for white girl) doesn't know the answer". It was bad enough she was the chaperone for my cabin at 5th grade camp. I lost my voice when we had to do skits and she decided our cabin would do an anti-smoking skit that was no fun at all, and I refused to participate. It was time to go.

A FEW HAUNTINGS

After a short visit with my grandparents and the coldest summer we had ever experienced south of San Francisco, we settled in San Jose for 6th grade. Having gone to 8 schools by now, I had developed a familiarity with a sick stomach on the first day of school. So much so, that a few months after school started, I had a sick stomach one morning, and I told my mom that I thought we were getting a new kid in my class because I had a sick stomach like the first day of school. I think she just looked at me like – *that's interesting honey.*

Sure enough, to my amazement, standing in line outside of class getting ready to go in for the day was a new girl in line. I told my mom, and somehow it did not seem like a huge surprise to her. It was just a knowing I had.

Then we were off to Delano, and Lake Tahoe, and even rented a camper and drove to Canada for a great family adventure. By seventh grade we landed in Virginia Beach, Virginia. We rented a little house in the suburbs, and I was now the oldest of four kids and the only girl. We made friends with our neighbors and everything seemed great. Then we had some odd things start to happen in the house.

One day the eldest of my brothers who was ten or eleven at the time, was in the garage by himself. He had been making some models. He had an electric football game set where the little plastic football player pieces would vibrate across the board. He kept the players in a clear plastic bag. He was extremely finicky about his things and notoriously would not share with me. He would tease me and say he would share, but I had to rent it from him. So I never borrowed his things.

Each player had a sticker on its back with the number of the player. No two were alike. Then I heard him scream from the garage. This was extremely rare. I'm not sure I had ever heard him scream about anything in his whole life.

He was a very level headed, science oriented kind of boy. My first thought was that he must have hurt himself on something in the garage. I ran out there, expecting to have to be ready to give him first aid of some kind, but he looked ok. I asked him what he was yelling for. He pointed to the plastic bag of his football players on a shelf on the wall in the garage. I looked over and just saw a bag of players.

He was holding a player in his hand. It had the number 16 on it. He said he had heard a rustling noise, and he saw his bag crinkling up on its own. He noticed the player number 16 in the bag appeared to be moving, and it inched its way up to the top of the bag amongst the other playing pieces.

Phil said he grabbed the bag and put the number 16 down in the bottom of the bag. Again, the number 16 player piece began to wiggle and move up to the top of the bag until finally it fell out of the bag and onto the floor where he picked it up and was now holding it.

The look on his face was a combination of upset, anger, confusion and shock. I had never seen him look like this before. And I believed every word. He was a very rational guy. He never screamed about anything before ever. It was extremely unusual.

Other things happened. My brother had made a miniature pool table out of cardboard and construction paper. He used marbles for the pool balls, and a bread wrapper tie he formed into a triangle for the ball rack. One day he was playing with it and got frustrated and he crumpled the ball rack into a tiny ball and threw it in the trash.

The next day the rack was perfectly formed and back in his room on the pool table. He came out of his room asking "who did this?" thinking someone played a joke on him. It could only have been my dad or me, but neither of us knew he had thrown the rack in the trash. Our two younger brothers were too little to be able to do anything like that, at only one and two years old. And my mother didn't seem to be paying enough attention to our little details to have any involvement. Mom had her hands full with my two youngest brothers who were under the age of two.

Then my mother started to hear a little girl calling "Mama". She was in the kitchen washing dishes and turned around to see a little girl about 3 or 4 with blond braids standing there, and she called out "mama". As if all this wasn't enough, I heard footsteps going around my bed at night. There was an antique night table that had been left behind in the house.

It was the night before Christmas, and we did not have a tree that year, and we put our gifts on top of this little night table. My parents had cut out a tree shape of astro turf and hung it on the wall above the night table. This was unusual to say the least, but we were pretty broke and it was better than nothing. I had bought a little Chinese wind chime for my mom in the school holiday gift shop. It sat amongst the modest gifts on the table. Apparently one of the table legs was shorter and the table would jiggle if bumped.

The kids were all in bed for the night and my parents were finishing wrapping presents when they started to hear a jingling noise. It was coming from the table. The chimes I had wrapped were tinkling as something was tipping the table. There was nobody around it.

My mom didn't know I was giving her chimes, and so the sound confused them a little bit since my gift was wrapped. In the morning when she unwrapped it she told me what had happened. We thought it must have been the little girl who had appeared who had moved the table. We later learned that a family who had lived there lost a little girl to illness.

My middle brother was two years old and he seemed unusually aware for his age. One time he read a sign that said "no drinks allowed", and he told my mom he knew what it was like to be in a coffin and he had been a cowboy in a rodeo and died. We were amused and wondered if he was having past life memories. There was nobody in our family who was a rancher or rodeo rider and we didn't live near anything like that. It came out of the blue from him.

THE PLAYFUL DEAD

The next year we moved to military housing in Norfolk, Virginia. I was still having periodic "smell visits" from my great grandfather. They usually came out of nowhere and just stayed long enough for me to notice it and a moment or two later it would be gone.

I was outside in our yard trying to plant some flowers by the side of the house. I was squatting down, and suddenly his smell came to me, and an image in my mind of an old black and white photo of my grandmother that must have been taken in the 50s, in her garden in the exact same position that I was in!

I remembered having seen that photo. And then BOOM! I was knocked on my butt.

My left leg had come up and thrown me off balance by some kind of force. I did not fall from just losing my balance, something pushed my leg up enough that I would lose my balance. It all happened so fast. Immediately, I ran in the house to tell my mom what had happened. Mom said her grandfather had taken that photo of her mother, and he was probably just playing with me. I could not believe it!

I felt a surge of excitement run through me. I was pushed over by a dead person. This was one of those stories that I ended up sharing with friends from time to time. I was as surprised as they were.

By the start of ninth grade we had moved to Bucks County, Pennsylvania. We rented a house while we waited for more affordable military housing to open up. The house was a brick townhouse in a nice suburban area. Pine trees surrounded the development. We enjoyed the ice cream truck that came onto our street at the end of summer, and I was able to start my babysitting career with several families in our neighborhood with small children.

I was happy that I was finally going to make some money, and my new best friend Karen lived across the street.

My mother became friends with the owner of the house we were renting. The woman had just recently been widowed, and moved out of the house because she wasn't comfortable being there for some reason, so she found somewhere else to live nearby with her son, but they came over now and then, since my mom became friends with her.

Then my mom started to tell us that weird things were happening. She found cigars in her shoes in her closet. My dad did not smoke cigars or even own them. But the man who died did. She would smell a waft of cigar smoke go by her, and she said she felt like someone was pinching her bottom at times when she walked around the house.

When we moved into the house it seemed that all the belongings of the owners had been removed. How could the cigars of a dead man get into my mother's shoes? It was a real mystery.

I was at school one day in P.E., learning to play basketball. My great grandfather's smell came around, right in front of me. It moved to my left side and as I tried to follow the smell, I had to lean my head to the side. Just as I did that, a basketball whizzed past my head on the right side.

If I had not leaned my head, I would have been hit square in the nose with that ball. I could not believe what had just happened. I felt as though I would have gotten a broken nose from that ball, and I was saved. I felt like someone was looking out for me.

MY FIRST PSYCHIC DREAM

Base housing opened up, and we moved to Philadelphia on base at the shipyard. It was 1976. An interesting time to live in Philadelphia. The city was celebrating the bicentennial, and racial tension was as high as ever. There were almost daily fights and frequent stabbings at school in South Philly, on the subway. There were metal bars on the windows at school and guards in the halls. It was a very fearful thing to go to school.

The schools looked scary on the outside, and the inside was the same. My younger brother Phil was jumped by four black guys one day and beaten up pretty badly. Racial differences were very real and even though we had nothing against them, we knew we were still at risk of being attacked. I was able to transfer to a little annex school a few blocks away from the main high school, but we still had to go there for

P.E., and the locker room racial stress was scary as well. I got stared at by black girls in the locker room giving me threatening looks that said they didn't want me there. I was so scared by it, that I actually got an excuse from doctor to get out of P.E.

I missed my best friend Karen from my previous school very badly, and though there were kids my age in our new neighborhood, they were more immature and rough. I became a target of bullying by a group of girls on my street, and one day they waited for me at my bagging job outside the Commissary, waiting for it to close so they could gang up on me. They sent a mutual friend in to warn me that they were waiting for me after work. My parents were not home for me to call for help. I should have tried to go out a back door at the commissary but they were all locked by closing time.

At 15 years old, there were few things I had experienced that were at the level of this kind of social dysfunction. All because they didn't like that I was friends with a boy they liked and they wanted to control which females he could be friends with. After yelling at me for a few minutes one of them slapped me hard in the ear. I made a break for it and ran home.

I had been friends with her older sister and even had a sleep over at her house. It was a crazy pack mentality they chose to be part of. We called the police after my dad got home. Living on base carries strict rules for military dependents. The whole family could be forced to move off base if they don't follow the rules. But it hit me hard, and was something that kept me from becoming part of my own neighborhood.

My first recorded psychic dream was February 19, 1976. I dreamed I was in bed in my room and my brother showed up at my door with a friend of his. 24 hours later my brother was standing in my doorway telling me to get up and his friend Greg was right there with him, which was the first time he had ever had a friend over that early in the morning.

My dad went out to sea, and while he was gone my mother had a party with some of her friends from the neighborhood, and they hired a well-known psychic from New Jersey to come do readings. I was very excited about this. I asked if I could get a reading, but the answer was no, she only did readings for adults. I was not allowed to be in the room during the party, but when the psychic had finished after several hours of doing readings for everyone, I came upstairs from the basement and saw one woman leaving in tears.

I was told the psychic told her that her husband would have lung cancer. (He got tested and it proved to be true). The psychic was still there and she looked terrible compared to when she arrived. She looked tired and drained. I had never seen someone who was not doing some kind of physical activity change so much in physical appearance on their face like this, it was interesting.

Months later my dad came back from his cruise, and things started to fall apart between my parents. I found out that the psychic had told my mother that my father had cheated on her when he was out to sea. Whether he did or he didn't, it opened the flood gate, and they reached a point of no return very quickly. My mother moved out and I was left to help care for my youngest brothers. I didn't know where she had gone for a while. I had never cut school before, but I did then to go and try and find her.

I went to the house of a friend of hers I knew, and she was there. She got into another relationship right away, they decided to get married and we moved to Concord, California.

By this time, though it had been quite challenging to live through all the moves and school changes, and losing friends and most of my belongings, thankfully I kept all my letters and diaries and photos. I had experienced a vast array of culture in the United States from Boston to Hawaii, the inner city to rural isolation. Concrete to jungle. I had to let go of everything again and again, but I always had my family and a friend or two nice enough to keep in touch with me.

For many years afterwards I internally moaned and complained about the challenges. But I was not a victim. It was very educational, and I saw all kinds of humanity. More than if I have grown up in one house in one town all my life. Yet while I was going through it, I mostly projected resistance to it, and held onto that feeling all the way up until I was married and living in Okinawa.

Today, I see the gift buried in the chaos of never knowing how long we would stay in one place, or where we would go next. I learned resilience, and that life gives you as many chances as you can take. So keep trying. I don't feel like a survivor, because that puts it back in the victim status. I feel like I learned, and if there were difficulties there were also benefits along the way.

Arriving in Concord was one of the major benefits. I found high school there to be a total joy after what I had experienced in Philadelphia. Everyone was nice. There were no hooligans out looking for trouble, except in rare circumstances, and I made some really wonderful friends, and I liked all of my teachers. Most of my classmates had grown up together since elementary school, and they were relatively bored with each other in comparison to my excitement at being at a school where there were no guards, no gang activity, and everyone got along pretty well, and seemed focused on learning. I was about as happy as I had ever been.

OUT OF BODY EXPERIENCE WITH MOM

My mom just wanted to get back to California, and my new stepdad was up for adventure. After the long road trip to Concord, we moved in with my mother's parents. Which was not ideal by any stretch, but it was expensive to live out West and my grandparents were generous to help us.

My brother and I would go to the clubhouse in our neighborhood with our Papa and he would teach us to play pool. We walked to school together, and I was now in eleventh grade.

One morning I was walking to school with my brother and we reached a dirt road about a block away from school on the back edge of the school property. It was not quite a two lane road, but it had vehicle access. Up ahead coming toward us was a beat up old black sedan with 3 teenagers in it. The driver was showing off, and as he passed us he revved the engine. He drove a few yards behind us, and then he did a fast U-turn, and started driving toward us.

I looked to my left side. We were on the far right of the road. It seemed like more than enough room to my left. I heard a little voice in my head say "MOVE OVER". A real voice. Not just my own thinking. But I had just looked to my left, and I was sure there was more than enough room. I ignored it.

The engine got louder and louder, and he intentionally revved the engine. Then BOOM! I went down in the dirt on my butt. The front right fender had clipped me behind my left knee, and knocked me to the ground. Dirt flew up like a cloud. I breathed it in, and felt dirt on my tongue, and in my eyes. I felt dirt in my nose and lungs. I coughed, and tried to spit the dirt out.

I was covered in dirt. The car stopped. All three kids got out. I stood up. I didn't know what to do. I think I said "You could have killed me! A few inches more and I would have been under the wheel!"

The girl in the back seat started yelling at me "You don't think he did it on purpose do you!!!" I didn't say anything else. I took a look at the license plate XA**** (all these years later it is still burned in my memory- omitted here for the owner's privacy), and continued walking to school with my brother. I went to the nurse's office and asked the woman at the desk "what do I do if I was just hit by a car?" They had me lie down on a bed for a few minutes, and then released me to go to my classes.

Nobody called my parents. All day I was a broken record at school. "I was hit by a car today" ... again and again. Then I walked home from school. The second I set foot in the house, I collapsed and the pain in my leg became excruciating. It took a long time for my leg to heal, but luckily there were no broken bones. I was very lucky. I had heard a voice, and I didn't listen to it.

Upstairs in my room one day I was looking out the window onto the street in front of our house. Nothing was going on, but I felt myself in a different state of mind. It was almost as if everything got quiet and the world just floated away. In a flash I was downstairs in the kitchen watching my mom at the kitchen sink peeling potatoes to cook for dinner. But I wasn't. I was still in my room, and suddenly I was back in my body from viewing my mother downstairs.

I thought what the heck just happened? I had been looking out the window, not downstairs. I ran downstairs to the kitchen, and there was my mom, peeling potatoes.

Before the flash experience happened, I had no idea what she was doing. I told my mom what happened. She turned around and said that's weird, I was just upstairs looking at you looking out your window! Whoa. Well, to say that it was a goosebumps moment is an understatement. We were blown away.

The few friends that I shared this with didn't know what to make of it either, and I think I just tucked it away out of worry of what people would say. I was just happy to be at a good school with nice kids and I was so thankful to finish high school there.

My best friend Maureen and I made the questionable and unfortunate choice to get our hair permed like Barbra Streisand. I know for a fact it cost me some dates in high school, but Maureen and I had a great time going out dancing and being asked if we were twins when we were at school. My English teacher called me out on my hair one day when I was late to class, and said "Glad you could make it to class, Rat's Nest!" He was the most popular teacher at school, and even though it was humiliating, I still liked him.

Christmas of 1978 Maureen and I planned to exchange gifts with each other. She came over to my house one night for some holiday goodies and we were going to give each other our gifts. She opened hers first, and then I opened the one she gave me.

They were practically identical holiday colored footy pajamas. We laughed so hard. Of all the things we could have given each other and we picked out the very same gift.

We did almost everything together, we put in dozens of job applications for the summer around town together, and ended up working at the same pizza restaurant. We had a double date with my crush from work and his best friend Dave to see a terrible horror movie.

She was a great friend, and the reason I decided to go to Davis, because I knew she was super smart, and if it was good enough for her, it was good enough for me. I could not have been happier with the choice to go to Davis.

OUT IN THE WORLD

I started out at UC Davis as a psychology major. I had thought I would be interested in being a therapist, partly because I was so intrigued with psychology, but also, because my father's illness hit close to home, and I thought for a while I would be useful at it, and it would be gratifying to help people.

I really enjoyed the psychology classes and one year, Dr. Charles Tart was my professor for Abnormal Psychology. He was a leader in consciousness, parapsychology and spiritual psychology. Later on, I started seeing his name pop up in several books I was reading, referenced as an authority.

And here I had taken his class. I would have liked to have talked with him about some of my own experiences by then. His book The End of Materialism is a must read for skeptics, or those like me who were living with a skeptic (later on). I ended up changing majors and with nearly enough credits for a minor in Psychology, I finished with a degree in Design.

During college I was able to reconnect with my father's side of the family who lived just south of San Francisco. My grandmother had died while I was in high school, and I was disappointed to have missed the chance to meet her. My grandfather was still living, and he had already remarried to a long- time friend who was a former photo editor at Money Magazine.

I was able to visit a few times during my college years and saw my dad who was usually fairly medicated for his illness, and one of the few stretches of time that he was not hospitalized. It was hard to see him having a tough life, and feeling helpless to be able to do anything for him, while also having to accept the barrier to our having a normal father-daughter relationship. It was a blessing he was largely unaware of his situation.

During my visits to my grandfather's house, I would frequently smell a woman's perfume. It didn't seem to belong to his second wife. She had a different smell about her.

Years later, just before we moved to Okinawa, I took my kids to visit my grandfather. He came downstairs one day during our visit and he handed me two small jewelry boxes. He told me they had belonged to my grandmother and he wanted me to have them because I was their first grandchild. It was her wedding ring set and a sapphire bracelet.

I was overwhelmed, and it was incredibly meaningful to me to have something so special of hers. When we returned home, I wrote a note to my grandmother, telling her how much it meant to me to have her jewelry, and her needlework that my grandfather also gave me. She had done a lot of cross stitching in her life and had many beautiful framed pieces of needlework depicting wildlife like ducks in a lake and fruit.

The next day I was outside on the patio with my kids enjoying the sunshine in San Diego, and that familiar woman's perfume arrived and seemed to linger around my kids for a few minutes. I felt some chills go up my spine, but in a happy way, as I felt validation that the smell I was experiencing was in fact my grandmother whom I had missed the chance to meet.

Years later she would visit me again on my way to my first serious painting class in Rancho Santa Fe. Her perfume smell appeared in the car when I was about a mile away from my art teacher's house. The smell lingered for a few minutes. It made me feel validated that I was on a good path with developing my art.

The teacher there turned out to be fantastic and a real influence for many years.

After college, my long-time boyfriend who had just finished medical school asked me to move to Phoenix with him where he would be doing his internship. I wasn't really sure what I wanted to do yet, and I wanted to be near him, so I agreed to go. For my birthday we packed the car with a tent and some food and drove up to the White Mountain Indian Reservation. It was really beautiful, there was a stream and mountains.

We bought a camping permit and pitched our tent. There was nobody else there. After a little hike upstream we made a campfire, cooked some food, and just sat and watched the stars in the night sky. We were pretty tired and went to bed early.

Sometime during the night, I thought I got up to go outside the tent to go to the bathroom (or the potty spot a few yards back). I was too scared to walk in the dark to the outhouse 20 or 30 yards away. I sat down at the picnic table and I realized there was a woman there.

I knew my boyfriend was still sleeping inside the tent. It was as if I knew who she was, but I had never seen her before. She sat there silently, and I yapped away telling her to be careful if she went back in the area where I had just relieved myself, so as not to step in it.

Then, in a flash, it was morning. I was inside the tent with my face mashed up against the fabric of the tent as if I had been trying to eat my way out of the tent. I was instantly confused by what I remembered. It felt so real.

But, how could that have been? Who was the woman? Why didn't she say anything? Why didn't I ask her who she was? Was it a dream? Was it an out of body experience? It felt like an out of body experience to me for sure.

I had too many questions. And I knew I couldn't share it with my boyfriend, he would not be interested in it at all. But I had told him some of the stories from when I was kid. He didn't believe any of it. And yet, we managed to develop a bond. As long as I didn't bring up these kind of experiences.

I found a job in a department store doing visual displays. For the time being I was thrilled. At least it was related to art and design. I had a quirky and petit little boss named Olivia who looked much like Coco Chanel. She was about fifteen years my senior, and a chronic chain smoker in the office, which I could barely tolerate (in those days smoking was allowed in the office).

She liked me right away, and we started taking our lunches together. I shared my odd childhood experiences with her and she suggested some books for me to read. I had read a lot about Dr. Elisabeth Kubler-Ross in college about death and dying, and even wrote a paper on her theory of the five stages of grief. I started to read books on psychic development, energy and some of it seemed to click.

Olivia was my first friend outside of my family who I could tell all of those things to, and for a while it was like she was a second mother to me. We were both reading some of the same spiritual books, and sort of had our own tiny reading club. We had a very strong connection, and I made a T Shirt for her before moving away that said High Frequency Thought on it, which was something we had joked about frequently.

Years later when I would contact her, she had just worn my shirt two days prior to my reaching out to her, even almost 30 years later! I could not believe she was keeping my T shirt that long, and though it lived in her closet barely touched for years, she managed to pull it out and wear it within 48 hours of my contacting her. The second time it had been nearly 20 years since we had been in touch at all.

After the Internship, we moved to Texas for my boyfriend's first job in the Navy, where we got married. And the next year our son was born shortly after we moved to San Diego, and my husband left for a 6 month deployment.

When I wanted to visit my grandparents in Northern California, my Papa flew down to drive up north with me and my son, so I wouldn't be alone on the ten hour drive to their home in Walnut Creek. I think after my mother's car accident when I was little, he was especially cautious about women in the family driving. He drove back home with me and then flew home. In 1990 our daughter was born, and three months later my beloved Papa passed away at the age of 80. He had been the sweetest man to me in my life.

THE AWAKENING BEGINS

By 1993 we had bought our first home, just as my husband was finishing his medical residency. He came home one day and told me we were going to have to move to Okinawa, and for me, it seemed to open a Pandora's Box. My first reaction was utter heartbreak. With the stress of his residency, and just sheer lack of time at home, we were struggling to get along, and we went long stretches without even speaking to each other. It was not healthy or happy.

I had moved so many times already, I just could not comprehend moving to the other side of the planet, and giving up pets who were family members for a man who barely seemed to care about me. Plus his mother was very sick with terminal cancer. I just didn't see how I could do it. We had more pets than we were allowed to take. We had a dog and four cats. There was a two pet limit.

I think I snapped. Things started happening again. I started keeping a dream journal on October 19, 1993. The following month I decided I wanted to go to a therapist for marriage counseling. I was given a referral on November 8th by a therapist who was the wife of a colleague of my husband's. She had done an internship with this therapist and she felt he was a good choice.

I started going for sessions with Harry in Solana Beach on October 12, 1993. He was Jewish and from the East Coast. I felt comfortable talking to him at his office adjacent to his home where he lived with his family, and he seemed to be fully present during our sessions, supportive and competent.

On November 8, I finally began to take notice of the décor in his office. He had a few items that suggested interest in a variety of spiritual teachings, Buddha statue, a few interesting knick knacks, and a large framed print of Machu Picchu on the wall. I asked him if he had ever been there, and it started a conversation that lead to him telling me about his *"integrative therapy"*, which involved looking into a patient's immediate past life for any traumas or issues that might be causing difficulty in this life.

Harry shared that when he was a teenager he had a premonition about the assassination of President Kennedy, and this had set him on a path to investigate the nature of reality and metaphysics.

Well this was new to me. I had never imagined he had such an esoteric background. Certainly the friend who had recommended him would have known, yet she never said anything. Neither she nor her husband seemed to have an interest in anything beyond accepted science, just as my husband did not.

I was absolutely shocked, and I had a very dramatic response to this news. My jaw dropped, I clasped my face with my hands, I gasped out loud and then began to laugh. It was almost as if I couldn't get away from this stuff. No matter what I did, it was following me everywhere.

Living with a serious skeptic, I was walking both sides. I was having unusual experiences, but I was still trying to do things to placate my husband's sense of science. So when I picked the person to request a therapist referral from, it was someone I thought was holding a similar belief system to my husband, and this outcome was completely unexpected.

Then I discovered there was a partial connection in the first dream I had recorded on October 19. *"I was with a man from the east coast who was Italian or*

Jewish, he was some kind of psychic. My jaw dropped as if I was in shock that maybe he really was psychic and I know my face was expressing amazement and he noticed I was looking surprised". So I had the dream after I met him, but before I was introduced to his real method of therapy and the news that he had his own psychic experiences.

I shared some of this with my husband one night and he took a long walk around the block and came home and said "if this is what you believe, then I don't think I can stay married to you". He clearly thought I was a nut job. It was a dark and sad feeling. You know what your own experience is, and it's like the person you should connect with most in the whole world is shutting you out, and making you feel like a fool, like I was not even intelligent anymore. Yet, this was part of the core of my being. If he had even just tried to have an open mind about it, the whole dynamic of our relationship would have changed dramatically for the better.

I decided I wasn't going to go to Okinawa with him. I reasoned he could come home and visit us, and it would shorten his time there to two years instead of three if we went with him. He left without us, and put our family on the waiting list for base housing, just in case I changed my mind.

After three months, he called with an emotional plea and talked me in to going. I had never heard him so emotional, and it touched me deeply. I could see that he missed us all very much, and having any kind of emotional expression from him was all that I wanted.

Then, one of our cats was killed by a coyote, and I found a great home for our two year old Samoyed dog Sierra. That left three senior cats who I could not bear to rehome. He was able to get permission to bring three cats.

He called and said he had a house for us, and I needed to learn Japanese. I was terrified. I could not imagine that we would do well over there. And I worried about how I was going to get around. This was like the mother of all moves for me. I had gone to fourteen schools and moved almost every year until college. I should have known how to do it, but emotionally I was exhausted from it.

I signed up for a one on one Japanese tutor to try to start on some basics of Japanese. It was not going to be easy. I felt a lot of distress internally, it was like the first day of school every day all over again.

I was having vivid dreams, and was pretty diligent about recording them. I was reading everything I could get my hands on, trying to learn how to make sense of these mysterious things that were happening.

One day in the bookstore, some books fell on the floor in front of me by Maya Angelou. *I Know Why The Caged Bird Sings*. I thought to myself, well isn't that the truth!

I had a strong sense that something pushed them as a message. I know things can fall over, but this was really more like someone knocked them over intentionally in front of me. In a way, I felt like it was speaking to what was going on with me. The pressure of the upcoming move had unlocked some kind of energy and things were taking off with a life of their own.

November 9, 1993, During the day I was experiencing the smell from my counselor's office. It became stronger around 5 pm and lingered until past 8:30. This was the longest period of time I had ever experienced a smell event. Around 6 pm the smell was so strong I almost called my therapist on the phone. A neighbor girlfriend of mine Jenny, who was a police officer called to tell me that she had arrested my youngest brother James on felony drug possession, and he was facing several years in prison. I was extremely upset.

My brother was in his early 20s. I had been trying to help him. He didn't have a car or a job. I had recently given him my bike from college. I couldn't bear the thought of him going to jail. Just the day before Jenny had told me "I hope to God I never have to arrest him", but here she was 24 hours later having done just that. I felt as if she had purposely set out to do that. What the smell of my counselor's office had to do with this, I'm not totally sure, but he was at the very least a resource to talk things over with, and I needed someone to talk to.

My dreams began to have a theme. They were suddenly all about spiritual growth and being taught by guides and teachers. I was introduced to a woman and a man who were in business clothes and it was their job to help me. They were preparing me to deal with knowledge about spirits.

I started to dream about abstract symbols, and I tried to draw them in the journal whenever I could. I didn't understand any of it but I drew it anyway. I saw a cluster of five rounded rectangles with sky inside each of them with tiny bubbles lining the rim of each oval, I saw metal carvings in bronze or gold on large tablets.

In November my middle brother came down from Los Angeles for a visit. When he arrived we were visited by a couple of spirits that we could sense a strong vibrational charge in the house, possibly to listen to my brother and I discuss my dreams, and we were going to use the Ouija board. To explain how

I knew they were there, I can only say if you close your eyes in a room with other people, and nobody is talking, you have a sense of space being filled up in the room, it's a little bit like that except that they weren't necessarily standing on the floor the same way that we were. I saw a spark of light up by the kitchen cabinets.

Shortly after he arrived though, my brother smelled cigarette smoke in the house, and became suddenly frightened and said we had a bad spirit in the house. It was a non-smoking household. I didn't smell the smoke, but I did smell a man's foul body odor, that was not at all related to my brother.

My brother had recently become a Born Again Christian, and he called his roommate in LA to pray for my house. He insisted we burn the Ouija board in the fireplace. I thought he was really over reacting, but his level of fear had raised my own discomfort enough that I agreed to burn the board. Neither of us could sleep until about 5 am. The next day after my brother left, I was taking a shower while my kids napped, and the heavy male body odor I had smelled earlier came into the bathroom with me. I had never had that happen before, and it was a rare time that I was actually frightened in the day time.

This was the first time I decided to burn sage in the house to try to clear the bad energy. I didn't like the smell of sage, but the house seemed to feel much calmer after I finished, and the male smell did not return.

I took my kids to visit my paternal grandfather for a few days near San Francisco. While we were there my grandfather came downstairs one day during our visit and he handed me a small jewelry box. He told me it had belonged to my grandmother and he wanted me to have it since I was their first grandchild. It was her wedding ring set and a sapphire bracelet. I was overwhelmed, and it was incredibly meaningful to me to have something so special of hers.

When we returned home, I wrote a note to my grandmother, telling her how much it meant to me to have her jewelry, and needlework that my grandfather also gave me. She had done a lot of cross stitching in her life and had many beautiful framed pieces needlework depicting wildlife like ducks in a lake and still lifes. The next day I was outside on the patio with my kids enjoying the sunshine in San Diego, and that familiar woman's perfume arrived and seemed to linger around my kids for a few minutes. I felt some chills go up my spine, but in a happy way, as I felt validation that the smell I was experiencing was in fact my grandmother I had missed the chance to meet.

Then for Thanksgiving, I drove up north again with the kids to see my maternal Grandma.

She gave me a few of my Papa's things. A sweater of his and some photos. On the trip home, we had just gotten on the freeway south and were approaching a hill that I couldn't see what was on the other side. Suddenly in the car in front of me was a waft of the **distinct** smell of my Papa. I can't describe it, I just had no doubt in my mind it was his smell.

This was my first time experiencing his spirit smell in the three years since his death. I had a mix of emotions. I was happy, I was sad, I missed him very much. But I also knew if he was visiting me in the car, there was a reason. Because he always cared about my car travels.

I reached the top of the hill and suddenly there was dead stop traffic on the other side. The road was jammed for what looked like miles. We basically sat stopped for nearly an hour before traffic started to move. I would have given anything to talk to him. I started to cry. It was a very powerful feeling to know he was still with me somehow, even though I didn't know how to communicate with him, he was able to show me he was there at a time that meant he was watching out for me too. At that point, it was one of the most intensely emotional experiences of my life.

I dreamed that my husband was able to come home for a week and help us move to Okinawa. A week later I got a call from him with the news he would be able to come back and help with the move. This had been in doubt and I thought I was going to have to do it alone with the kids and animals. We had to sell the car, put everything in storage, rent out the house, and we would fly out of Los Angeles in February.

The next day I dreamed about seeing two women wearing full length fur coats. I felt how soft they were. One was supposedly made of Beaver. I read the newspaper in the morning and saw a story about two stolen fur coats from Saks Fifth Avenue at Fashion Valley Mall. I didn't think this had anything to do with me, other than to show me I was making new connections in my dream time that even related to the news, and it was new and mysterious to me. I did not own a fur coat, and would never want to own a fur.

Then another dream had a voice without a body giving me information about learning to access ancient information. I awoke in the morning to find my right arm and hand reaching up and making specific and absolutely gorgeous choreographed dancing motions, it looked very professional, and it literally blew my mind to watch it because it was not something I had ever tried to do myself. I was told I would eventually know how to use it and then the word Aquarius was spoken. (I did not know much about astrology at this point beyond the typical classic characteristics that are usually associated with each sign, and even then I was only aware of the signs of my immediate family, and none of us were Aquarius). I tried to move my arm the same way and could not. It was like a Balinese hand dancer. I had never been particularly coordinated or graceful. The grace I witnessed in my hand motions were unlike anything I had ever done.

Later that day I was in a spiritual bookstore with my kids. While I was browsing through books, my four year old son had gone off to look at something, and he came back and asked me "what is four and four?" I replied "eight, why?" He said "I wanted to know how many arms that lady had", and he pointed to a poster on the wall of a goddess dancer with eight arms. She was doing motions very much like the arm movements I had experienced that morning.

Known as Devi, Mother-Goddess, Divine Mother, Goddess Shakti. I really didn't know any of the mythology behind it at the time. I had not read anything about her before, but the timing seemed connected to what happened to me that morning. I mean, if you are having some of these kinds of things happening to you, it only seems natural you might try to seek out more information about it which is why I went to the bookstore, but before that morning, I had no mental connection to the woman on the poster.

Though when my son pointed to it, it was a big *wow moment.* In a way, it felt as though I was on some kind of treasure hunt, and I didn't even know it yet. Like I was being given hints in advance, and then sent on my way to stumble upon these mini a-ha moments. *I was told in a dream that I was being shown something worldly.*

December 17th, *I dreamed I saw a man with long white hair and a white beard. An old man like the image of* ***God.*** *He told me to "remember the number 74". To record it, that I hadn't recorded it when I should have, and that I should do it now. I was told to "****write it down****".* The idea that he could be ***God*** did not register with me, but he was definitely an authority figure, or master teacher. Basically he just appeared to me in a dream with no introduction, and I asked no questions at that time. Later I had a thousand questions. What is 74? Why do I need to remember it? Who are you? When will I see you again? Is that how long I will live? Is someone going to die at 74? How can you tell me 74, and no further information? On and on.

Today I have some mixed feelings about sharing this. I can't be sure, but I think it could play out in

2016. It's not something yet where I can say "see how this one turned out", but the dream itself was on the level of having a big impact on my taking my dream journals more seriously, and gave me a sense of having a serious teacher figure who was guiding me.

When you are having dreams come true with trivial information, and then someone with some apparent authority, or wisdom shows up who might even be **God**, it might be nice to get more information than I was getting. I tried to question most things with a student's mind. But I did not have much patience. I wanted to know everything right now. Apparently that is not how all of this works.

TIME

In January on my mother's birthday (the 11th), I was awake late at night and walking down the hall from my room into my son's bedroom to comfort him. I very clearly heard a male voice in my head say *"Lay down with your children. You will be able to continue the Master's teaching after the death of (husband's name)"* This actually frightened me. It was vague, and it concerned me for my husband's safety.

But I also realized that it could mean other things beyond a physical death, if our relationship ended, that would be like a death if he left my life. It was also confusing because it seemed to contradict my instruction to write it down. I really wanted more clarity than this. It seemed confusing to have just received a message from the *"master teacher"* recently, only to now be told that the teaching would *"continue after the death of (husband's name)"*. Maybe there would be lower teachers guiding me for a while.

My husband's belief system, and outright objection to what I was getting into, was a clear issue. He had a right to his beliefs. I wasn't willing or ready to give up on our relationship, even though I wasn't exactly finding the right ways to connect with him, a feeling began to grow that there had to be a way to show him that what I was experiencing was real. I had this idea that if I could prove to him there was more than what he currently believed in the nature of reality, that it would bridge that gap between us, and bring us closer. I wanted more acceptance.

Fast forward to the time of writing this book and doing more reviews of the journals, inexplicably each time there is something new that had gone undiscovered previously. This time, the revelation that my husband's father had the *same name*, which of course was not a surprise to me, but he was a senior. My father in law of the *same name* passed away on January 11, 1999. This dream was 5 years to the day before, and mentioning his death by name!

I don't know how this piece of information never dawned on me until now, but I expected the voice to be telling me about something closer to me than my father in law I guess.

This year I have been in touch with two psychic mediums and both of them told me my former father in law is one of “my people” (without being prompted, they each brought up his name on their own). Meaning, he is one of my guides trying to look out for me, and he is looking out for my son as well, and his children and grandchildren, I would imagine. This point goes to show the **importance** of writing down the date of the dream or experience. Because you never know how long it may take you to sort things out down the road when things play out. And the date can be more important to the information of the dream than you might know at the time. Not always, but frequently it plays a role.

Time is a big aspect of dreams. There are so many questions that I don’t have the answer to about time and the nature of reality. But in my experience reviewing over 2000 dream pages of my own, the one thing I was meticulous about was recording the date. This showed me some interesting things.

In the precognitive or spiritually based dreams, many times the date was part of a message that was not apparent in the dream necessarily.

Sometimes the psychic dreams played out the same day, at 3 days or 7 days and frequently a month to the day. Sometimes dates were mentioned in the dream as a message for someone else. It gave a sense of when in the dream world being part of a mysterious clock and calendar without being too aware of it in the dream, it was by recording the date, and seeing how things played out later that I saw the connection. Now this could just be my personal mode of experience with these things, but I would bet that others will experience similar circumstances as well.

There have been other time connections that "spontaneously" appeared, and I guess those would be synchronicities. Before completing this book, I have been reviewing old books of mine that I have not looked at in years. Yesterday I picked up a Seth book and decided to take a look. The **first** page I opened it to was on psychic dreams. I read a couple of Jane Roberts' own psychic dreams, and I noticed that the first one I read was dated October 17, as I sat there reading it on October 18th. It caused me to feel a little more in sync by that unexpected similarity. After reading more of the book I would say there is some relationship there, even if it does on the surface sound sketchy.

I'm not saying I'm connected to Jane Roberts or Seth, but I am saying the date contributes to my sense of being aligned, and that I'm doing the right things. At least I'm trying to.

OKINAWA AND THE SPIRIT VORTEX

The day finally arrived that we were traveling to our new home in Okinawa, where we would live for almost three years. After the long 15 hour flight on a military plane we landed on Kadena Air Base.

The island was green and tropical surrounded by pristine aqua-blue Ocean. Our house was on base and just a short drive from the air field in the officer housing tract. My husband had already set up the house with base furniture.

We were all exhausted after a fifteen hour flight, and ready to rest at the new house, but my husband had to work the night shift at the hospital. After I got the kids into their beds, I decided to get some sleep myself. At exactly midnight, the thick and heavy interior window screen frame which was right over the bed, fell off the wall and hit me on the head. I panicked, thinking there was someone outside the window trying to break in. It was dark and I couldn't see much outside. But after a few minutes I realized there was nobody outside.

I tried to reattach the screen frame to the window. And inside I wondered what really made it fall off at exactly midnight. It was a scary introduction to my new home.

A few weeks went by and I was busy getting the kids situated in their new schools and trying to make some friends before I did much exploring, even on my own street outside of our house. While visiting my new friend Ruth, the mother of my son's classmate Ryan, who just lived up the street from us, she asked me a very funny question. She said "how do you like living on that street?" Her question surprised me, and I was puzzled. I asked her what she meant by that. Our street was a little circle of 8 houses surrounded on one side by jungle and a small volcanic mountain covered in dense vegetation.

To the right of our house was a row of hedges, the only separation between our neighbor's house and her very large grassy lawn where my kids played with her three boys almost every day.

In the middle of the circle was a memorial to something from World War 2. There were many memorials around the island, I hadn't looked at it yet, and I hadn't given it much thought. (Which in hindsight seems rather odd to me, but I was in a bit of a fog mentally when we arrived, and overwhelmed with the culture difference, and I hadn't arrived with the best attitude).

Ruth continued, "Your street marks the location of the Japanese surrender of the Okinawan islands. There have been many reports that some of the houses on your street are haunted!"

I felt the blood start to drain and chills raise up on my arms. It was as if I was just being told that if I thought anything I had experienced while growing up was something, I was going to be in for it now, and how ironic that my disbelieving husband had signed us up for this!

I felt confirmation that the screen falling on my head the first night in the house was no accident. I left her house and started walking back to mine. I felt like I was going to have to see what I was dealing with now.

I reached the court and turned right onto it, directly facing the memorial in the center of the street. As I approached it, chills raised up on my whole body.

I was standing in front of the memorial which marked the Sept. 7, 1945 surrender of the Japanese forces on Okinawa to the Americans, which also marked the end of World War II. The quote on the memorial read: "Dedicated by the United States Air Force 30, March 1964 to the importance of **Everlasting Peace and Understanding Among All People of the World**".

Soon after, we would see tour buses come on our circle to see the memorial, which always felt a bit like we were living on hallowed ground, especially when getting groceries out of the car in front of a small Japanese tour group. A year after we left, it was renovated into a Peace Garden with another plaque and quote: "The price of war is blood, but the price of peace is higher"-(Capt. Rhon Say).

To say my mind was blown is a total understatement! I felt the significance of this place, the people, and the spirit to my very core, as if my bones had just downloaded all of the history of this place. I was amazed (and not) that my husband didn't say anything to me about it before hand, or even in the couple of weeks that we had already been in the house. In hindsight I think he was trying to stay away from anything to do with spirit, even though he just placed us in a massive spirit vortex. And actually, it was probably no accident. It was perfect. Unfortunately, it only made my husband think I was even crazier.

So I decided I was going to settle in to this strange place and see how it goes. There was certainly no shortage of nice people, the wildlife and culture were also very beautiful and interesting. And yet, it ended up taking me an entire year to adjust to being there. We made many wonderful friends during our time there, and all these years later it is one of my fondest memories.

I went to bed that night on the left side of the bed (which would become my side while we lived there), and in the morning I was wakened by a man's voice in my right ear saying "Hi-Ya Chicky-boo!" It was American with an east coast Bronx type of accent. – There was nobody there. I knew it was a greeting of "*we know **you know** we are here*" type of thing. Ok, this is going to be interesting! Lots of dead soldiers around who know they can talk to me. I really am not used to this kind of thing, and while I suppose I was a little freaked out by it, I didn't feel like I was in danger, or my family was in danger, and I was just going to continue with my dream journals and keep track of everything.

This was at the very early dawn of the internet in 1994. We had a computer and Compuserve (one of the early internet providers). I was able to connect with my favorite author Richard Bach because he was intrigued that an American living in Okinawa (on an air base) would contact him. He had written about contacting himself in the future and other esoteric concepts that I found intriguing, and I tried to share with him some of what I was going through, though I imagine his main curiosity was that I was living on an Air Force base in Asia. None-the-less it was an exciting way to interact with my author idol.

I BEGAN TO HAVE WAR DREAMS

I was in a Japanese bomb shelter. It looked like a square tent that was hard with windows. I knew the war was going on outside, and someone was deciding to get rid of us. I had seen a bomb dropped and the target was disintegrated. I knew a bomb was going to be dropped on us and we would be evaporated. If we ran outside we could be shot. I was the only one in the shelter who knew we were going to be killed, and I thought at least we could all be together. The bomb was dropped and there was a bright light and I was waiting for us to die, and leave our bodies, but we didn't die. The bomb hadn't worked, and though we were nervous about it they didn't try again.

Needless to say, this felt totally real. I was there. This was me, and I was Japanese. If not me, I was experiencing someone else's reality. While my ER doctor husband got up in the morning to go to work, and I got up to get the kids off to school. I hastily scribbled down my dreams every morning in my journal before getting out of bed.

Frequently my husband would get the kids up before I got out of bed, and I felt guilty, but I had to write these things down or they would evaporate into the ether. And thankfully, my husband never verbally complained about this. I think he understood this was important to me, even if he didn't agree with it or understand it.

I could hear my kids talking while I wrote, either complaining about getting up or fussing with each other. Sometimes they would come and climb on top of me while I was trying to write quickly. My knees bent while sitting up in bed, and my three year old daughter was using my legs as a slide.

A dream from the American side:

There was a small American hometown headquarters where family member and girlfriends would check in to see if there was any word on the soldier they were concerned about. There were a few soldiers who were on a secret mission of some kind, and they had come back close to the headquarters without telling anyone, but were still carrying on the secret mission. They were hiding near bushes in a ditch outside and somehow they were never coming home and were going to die.

Those were intensely real feeling dreams. I felt the energy of war soldier spirits from both sides all around. I had dreamed the war from both sides. I had a strong sense that they knew I was aware of them, and in some ways they were playing with me. Then I would go about my business taking care of my family, and would return from shopping for groceries at the base commissary to see a tour bus on our little circle with a tour guide and microphone explaining the memorial in Japanese to tourists, while I pulled bags of groceries out of the trunk of my car, it was an odd feeling, as if we were living on sacred ground, and I was almost embarrassed that homes were built so close to this important memorial. But I guess it was also a strong example of how "life goes on".

The spirit world was quite active there reliving the war, and the modern day physical world was moving forward. There were a couple of times when my husband had to work at night and I felt a group of soldier spirits in the house, and I felt compelled to turn the tv on. We had one channel there, which was US Military. I turned the tv on and there was a documentary about the war on. I just let it play while I did my own thing. The power of this place was very strong.

THE OLD BOYFRIEND

A series of repetitive dreams regarding a past relationship began to pop up. There was a guy I had known in high school, and we were great friends. I had always had a crush on him, but nothing developed because I had dated his best friend, and there was some code of not dating your friend's exes. But in college, we started writing letters to one another, and continued as friends writing every month for five years. Then unexpectedly my college boyfriend (later husband) broke our relationship off for what turned out to be a year.

As soon as my friend heard that I was single, he offered a plane ticket for me to fly out and see him in Florida. He was possibly the greatest guy I had ever met. After a few trips out to see him, it looked like things were getting serious, although I didn't feel I could see how my life would fit with him completely.

But we had remained good friends, and I had the deepest respect for him. I stopped by one time for him to meet my kids on the way to visit family up north.

I think we had an unspoken agreement to stay friends forever.

Well, in March 1994, I began to dream of being on vacation at the same hotel in Hawaii as him. They turned out to be a year from the time it happened, 6 months, and a month before the date we were all at the same hotel on vacation on Oahu near my birthday. They were pretty similar. *The first one I asked him about his wife, and was he still with her. He said her name is Stephania and she was still around.* Well I thought that was strange, because that was NOT her name. And he was not still with his wife.

Two months before we went, I found out that he was going to be at the same hotel as us in Hawaii. We agreed to get everyone together and meet. He was taking his younger brother there on vacation. When we arrived, we left a message for him at the desk, and my husband and I took the kids out to the beach.

The kids began to play with some children from Brazil who were right next to us. There was a little boy named *Stephania*. This is where we were when my friend found us. We were with Stephania.

All of this blew my mind, and each "hit" made me want to do more and more. Yet, I was confused as to why some things were not very clear, and yet the detail was so amazing. Like why would he refer to his wife as Stephania, when we were with a little boy named Stephania. It was the name which was unusual (in my experience I had **never** met a Stephania before), combined with "she's still around", but could also work as Stephania is there with us.

One family member who considered herself somewhat of a spiritual teacher told me I was a powerful manifestor at the time. I didn't understand what she meant then, but when people and events come into our lives that we had dreamed about previously, on some level there has been a telepathic agreement at some point in time. Our thoughts, even our sleeping thoughts can create our reality.

I don't know how all of this works and what is involved to get a perfectly clear picture, yet having even these kind of bits delivered in a dream is still pretty exciting, and gave me a sense of being "onto something". I would later dream about his mother's death in 1999, oddly, two months after it happened. In the dream I was aware it happened two months previous. That may have been one of my rare dreams of knowing the recent past.

SOMETHING ABOUT MOM

Occasionally I had unusual vision dreams that clearly seemed to have some meaning, but are so abstract in nature they remain very confusing. It's as if they have their own language or code that has to be deciphered.

May 24, 1994, In one dream it was night time and I was in bed with my husband. We were awake (in the dream) and sitting up. We saw a blue rectangle floating at the foot of the bed. I knew it was my mother, and this meant she was dead. I thought my husband's mother was there too, but I couldn't see her. I reached out in front of me to touch my mom, and I tried to say "Mom" and I touched her hands in the middle of the bed, even though I couldn't see them, I recognized they were hers by touch.

I was crying out in my sleep and my husband woke me up. I felt very strongly upon waking, that this dream meant that my husband would come around to seeing what I see about life after death, once my mother passes away. I had very mixed feelings about including this, because as I write this my mother is thankfully alive and well. There was no time indicator that I was aware of, but the nature of the event convinced me some day something will be relevant to that vision.

THE SEARCH FOR PROOF

I think this dream about my mother contributed to my desire for my husband to have an open mind about the nature of reality and spirit, or at least be curious about exploring. And I decided to try to find a way to prove something to him.

I sent away for some meditation and self-hypnosis tapes. The recordings were designed to increase your receptivity to precognitive information during waking hours. While the kids were at school and my husband was at work, I began to try the meditations. The idea was to open up to whatever visions or information might come. And to try not to judge it. Just open up, relax and write down whatever information presented itself.

The goal was to find things that would happen within a three day time frame for a relatively quick turnaround time. I decided to go out on a limb and tell my husband what I was doing, regardless of whether it made me look like a fool or not. I decided it was worth the risk of looking stupid if I had any chance of proving something new to him.

On my very first try, I saw a very odd image. *I saw an arm holding a bare human spinal column.* I tried not to judge, and I told my husband about it right away. A day or two later, I was at our post office box. Our mail box was in the hospital where my husband worked, just around the corner from his department. So there I am at the box, and a man walks behind me and goes to his mail box a few feet away. He was wearing a T-shirt. He turned his back to me, and on the back of the shirt was a large image of a bare human spinal column and the words "Get a Spine!"

I gasped so loudly, he spun around to look at me, like "are you ok?" I stood there dumbfounded, while thoughts raced through my mind. I knew my husband was just around the corner, no more than 20 yards away. What was I to do? This guy looked at me with concern, and I realized I would sound like a lunatic if I told him my story. This was long before cell phones with cameras, and I didn't have my regular camera on me.

I felt completely stuck. I turned around and left. I got in the car and drove home, completely crushed.

I felt that there was no way I was going to be able to prove anything to my husband. And later when I shared what happened with him, his response was pretty much as I expected "well maybe you saw that T-shirt before at the mail box".

Was it possible? Anything is possible. But I didn't remember seeing it before, it felt very unlikely to me at the time. Maybe I should have kept trying for something else, but in reality my dreams that were coming true should have been enough. When someone is not interested in being ready or open to see things, I would think something very dramatic would have to happen to get their attention. I realized it wasn't my place to convince him. It just bothered me so much that this door was not going to be opened, and give us something to share. At the time, I had really felt that the fate of my marriage depended on this. We were hanging by a thread.

SPIRITUAL COMMUNITY SUPPORT

I decided to look for other people who had similar beliefs there, and found someone offering a meditation group. I saw a meeting at a cafeteria being held by a woman to discuss what types of meditation people might be interested in, and to decide who could host the meditation group meetings. Her name was Carol. She was a very fit blonde physical fitness trainer in her 50s. A man at the meeting named Joshua offered to host Sufi mediation groups at his house.

A few days later I was reviewing my dream journal pages and found this from four weeks before:

I dreamed I was at my house with a woman with blondish hair in my kitchen. She was there for two days and I didn't know who she was and I finally guessed her name to be Carol, and then I fixed some kind of food for her, and Carol took a bite and said "that food you gave me was all full of fat". The dream had her hair color, name and interest in healthy eating, specifically against "fat". Being a personal trainer was a match. In addition to the element of her being with me for a time with my not knowing who she was and I "guessed" her name psychically to be Carol, which is exactly what happened by having the dream about her four weeks before meeting her.

I started attending weekly meditation meetings at Joshua's house. Carol was there and Kelly as well as a few other people. We sat on the floor on pillows in a circle, and Joshua led the group with a chanted meditation. He had instructed that we bring rosary beads to help count the chants, and also recommended some books to read about a Sufi spiritual adventure by Reshad Feild.

He would start the meditation with In-Shala and then we chanted what meant all the names of God. " Al a la hee la, la hee la la", in a group it developed a rhythm of its own, and there was a lot of energy you could feel with this type of meditation. After a thirty minute meditation like this, I would frequently go home and have some amazing dreams that night.

Later on *I dreamed of seeing Joshua's astral body come to my house and pull me up out of bed and out of my body, and walk around my house together.* As if just to show me that it could be done.

Another time he told us we would have a weird dream, and I did. *I dreamed I saw a big yellow mattress floating in the air, and five black cylindrical vases with seven white flower petals falling into each vase. I saw a daisy with half of the petals off. My emotional response to these abstract images was of a pain in my stomach, and "oh no" feeling.* I told him about the dream and I said "see I didn't dream about you" and he said "but you did".

A month later in my Ikebana class I was assigned a flower arrangement with white daisies and half the petals were off. I felt the 5 vases were the people in the mediation group, and I learned that Joshua had been harassing one of the members for sex. I got sick, and felt the daisy was the time marker for when I would learn the news about the harassment and the "yellow bed".

Some dreams related to events that would develop on the same day. *In one dream I saw someone was planning to catch me and put me in a room with a giant snake so it would swallow me whole. It was terrifying. I believed I was going to be swallowed alive.*

Later that night my son chose a new animal book for a bedtime story that was in our book shipment and we hadn't read it yet. We turned to a page and saw a giant Anaconda. My 6 year old son asked me "Can a snake swallow a person whole?" It was interesting that in the dream I was the one who was potentially going to be swallowed alive, and I felt the fear and terror of being locked in a small space with a giant snake who could kill me. But then it presented itself in a zoological book of animals the same day, and it made me wonder what was going on.

It's one thing to have a dream about a snake and then see one the same day, but to include specifically "being swallowed whole" was very exact.

Another same day example was that *I dreamed about feet and legs of people having their bones broken. A man was breaking bones on other people. I imagined he broke the feet of everyone in the house and he was after me.* Later the same day my husband came home from work and told me about a young boy patient who broke his arm in two places.

My husband did most of his talking at work. When he came home, it was his time, and he rarely shared stories about patients. Partly out of privacy for the patients, but also because he wanted a break from it. I suppose in his job it was possible that he saw someone every day with a broken bone in the ER, but he rarely shared his cases with us. He was more inclined to share something if it made him think of his own family and kids. If this dream had not happened on the same day as what he told me, I would likely not be including it here since it wasn't a closer match.

In one dream there was something that happened that was almost re-enacted by my son just two hours later. I woke up at 5am after having a dream that really scared me.

In the dream a man in his boxer shorts got into the house and came here to get us. He was standing in our bedroom doorway and not saying anything. My husband and I woke up and I said "do something" to my husband. He said "You're out of uniform soldier!" "Where are your pants and your shirt? to the man, "Then he came over to my side of the bed creeping along the floor until he reached where my head was and I was so scared I backed across the other side of the bed over my husband and onto the floor. I got on the phone and didn't know whether to dial 911. I told the woman we had just been held captive for an hour by a man who worked for my husband. The man dashed out to his car and drove away. Two hours later my son snuck to the side of my bed just like the man in the dream, and it practically gave me a heart attack.

A few days later I woke up in the middle of the night and saw a beautiful sun face on the wall in my room. It was all white and 3 dimensional with a face in the middle. It looked like a ceramic wall hanging and all the points on the sun spires were curved and a little wiggly. The center was very rounded out. As my eyes began to focus on it I saw it dissolve and twirl like it was going down a drain into the wall. The drain material was made out of cloud or fog and it went into a hole. It looked like it was being flushed away. In the morning, I was visiting at Ruth's house, and she was looking at a catalog that had a white sun in it and she was thinking of me when she saw it. It was stationery with a white sun face on it. Later I saw a sun face bird feeder, which I ordered for the garden as a reminder of the experience, and it graces my garden fence even today.

During our time in Okinawa I studied Ikebana at the USO on Kadena, which was an ancient spiritually based art of flower design for two years with a wonderful sensei Mrs. Keiko Robbins. She was a master teacher and founding member of Okinawa Ikebana International in 1956. She impressed on the class the spiritual connection between people and nature. By the time we moved back to the states I would have finished an assistant teacher certificate and was given a flower name of *Kei Un*. Changing Cloud.

She was like a surrogate mother and grandmother to many of us military wives over there, bringing sweets to class for our children, and kindly critiquing our arrangements, encouraging us to keep it simple to enjoy the beauty of each flower. I dreamed I saw Mrs. Robbins and a long calm body of water with a lotus flower floating on top. I knew I was being shown that this was how my psychic abilities would develop. Slowly, over time, through the people I met and the places I go and things that I do. Not to rush it, it would happen slowly and it would be beautiful.

Two weeks later on vacation in Hawaii, I saw such a long body of water- a canal at the hotel we were staying at and visited a store called The Heavenly Lotus and I saw a T-shirt with the same artwork as the current dream journal cover (drawing of koi with leaves floating on water and tree reflection). I later learned that Mrs. Robbins had also gone to Hawaii around the same time.

A BAT RESCUE

While some dreams were more poetic and magical, a few were pretty straightforward. I enjoy both kinds, but it's certainly easy to appreciate a direct bit of information. But why the long wait for something seemingly trivial? Was it the wait, or was it what was relevant to what was happening to me?

In Okinawa we had a lot of bats. In fact our white sedan was parked outside under a tree with a lot of blue berries on them. Fruit bats would eat the berries and then their droppings would cover the car so much that we were always having to wash it off, and we jokingly called it the "bat mobile".

One day I was walking home at night from a friend's house. It was dark and there was a branch that stuck out over the sidewalk a bit. As I passed under it, a bat who had been resting in the tree bounced off of my head, and flew off. I was pretty startled and amused. It scared me for a split second until I realized what it was, I wasn't hurt and I was amazed there was a bat that close by. I think bats are adorable and look like little foxes. I was impressed by the vicinity of wildlife where we were living. I imagine this is why I picked up on the following dream.

April of 1995 *I dreamed about going out the front door and finding a baby bat between the screen door and the main door. I picked it up and set it free.* A year and a half later we had moved back to the states to a new home in San Diego, and one morning I woke up to find a baby bat stuck between the screen and sliding glass door to the back yard. I didn't know what to do with him and I hoped he would take off on his own. I put him on the patio table, but sadly I think another critter got to him. I have not seen another bat here since then.

IT'S A SMALL WORLD

May 12 1995 *I dreamed we had just gotten home and found that our things were in Howard Stern's house. And a tornado was heading right for it.*

Eight days later, we were at the Okinawan resort for military at Okuma with several of our friends and their kids for a few days. There was a *typhoon watch* at the time. One of the families brought a doctor friend visiting from the states. Nothing anyone said about him rang any bells, but I noticed he kept trying to get me in his photos he was taking during the day on the beach with all of us. There was an odd tension. Later we were all having dinner together, and I asked him where he was from. He said Danville, California. I mentioned the name of a good friend of mine who is from there, and he said Chuck is my best friend! It turned out 16 years before that Chuck and I and this guy with the last name **HOWARD** had been on a double date with my best friend Maureen. In fact we went to see the movie Phantasm, which was a gory horror film, and not much fun for my girlfriend and I. He shared that he had actually watched that movie again just a couple of days prior, which seemed like an extra odd coincidence.

My face turned red and I laughed so hard I choked on my margarita. Everyone laughed. What are the odds of that? We were all stunned at what a small world it was, and I had no memory at the time, of a dream with a Howard and storm headed right for us.

June 25, 1995 *I dreamed I was at a grocery store at the checkout counter and I discovered I did not bring my checkbook but somehow I had won a specific amount of money, and I paid with that, and they gave me the change which I put in my pocket.* July 25, 2011 my natural father died, and I inherited the same amount of money as in the dream. I had not seen him in a few years. He had spent the majority of his life after my mother divorced him, in mental hospitals, and he lived one of the most tragic lives I have ever seen. I was thankful to have had the last two weeks of his life with him, so that he was not alone. I am still waiting for a time when I may reconnect with him.

July 4 1995 *I dreamed our friend in Okinawa, Marie told me about losing things.* 20 days later she told me her Hong Kong shipment of furniture purchases had been lost.

July 6, 1995, more same day events- *I dreamed I was at a Japanese store. It had some beads and the sales lady was showing me some pink amethyst beads that were up on a shelf. There were people putting skates on right next to me.*

First thing in the morning, Danny from next door showed up at the house with his roller skates on. He took his skates off right next to me in order to come in the house. Later in the day Carol took me to the flea market and I saw lots of beads there.

Second dream on same day (long range): *My husband and I were at church sitting in pews waiting for something. Our friend Chris said they had good food there. It was an all you can eat buffet, and that's what we were there for. A preacher started to speak, and we were just wondering when we were going to get to eat.*

My husband was an atheist, and we had never gone to church together during our marriage or any other time. In 1998 I brought my husband to the church I had just started going to for the first time. They had a special night time event with a dinner planned. He came right after working a 12 hour day, and was starving. But it turned out to be a learning lesson, rather than an actual dinner.

We arrived, and in the main sanctuary area there were a few tables on one side of the room that had table cloths, candles and place settings. To the other side of the room was open floor space. People were randomly selected for either tables or floor, with the majority of people getting the floor. The number of people represented the percentage of hungry to wealthy people in the world. We were in the group to sit on the floor.

The people selected for the tables got a full dinner served and we only got a small bit of rice as a lesson about world hunger, we saw a video on the big screen with statistics. It was called the **Hunger Banquet,** which we were told after we had arrived. It was a simulation to demonstrate the imbalance of food distribution around the world.

After having worked all day at the hospital and being told we were having dinner there, it was probably the only reason he agreed to go. He was not amused, and he never came to church with me again.

I realize now that this one event could have been some proof for him because it involved him specifically. I'm not sure I made the connection back then to dream. I wasn't regularly reviewing my journals, and this one was almost 3 years earlier.

Another thing I noticed after reading about Jane Roberts' psychic dreams was that she said if she had a psychic dream one day and had any other dreams on the same day, they all tended to be psychic. I would say that is also the case for me. But what is interesting is that I could have a same day dream AND a long range dream on the same day about very different things. It makes me feel like I was bouncing around quite a bit.

August 5, 1995 *I dreamed my husband and I were traveling back to a place we had been to before and we saw the hotel we stayed at when it was brand new. We saw the room we had stayed in. We were walking past the hotel to my husband's father's house. On our way back we saw a kind of gambling machine and he put a coin in and it kept adding up and I didn't know how much he won.* August 9- We were staying at the resort at Okuma. My husband won 45 nickels in a slot machine at the restaurant after we walked past the first room we ever stayed in. He ordered a gin and tonic just like his dad used to drink, which he never did, and he said he was missing his dad.

I was having some concerns about my grandmother back in the states. She had emphysema and had to carry an oxygen tank with her everywhere. She was now in her 80s and it was tough for her to get around on her own. She didn't drive a car and had to take public transportation. November 25, 1995 *I dreamed I saw my grandma at her place and I saw my aunt Ruth outside talking to people asking them not to tell my grandmother she was there because she wanted to surprise her.* A week later I found out my aunt was flying from Florida to see my grandmother and help her get to the hospital.

In December 1995 *I dreamed I was at a house with my grandparents. Papa was lying down on some kind of leather couch. It was more like two narrow twin beds that were attached. His bed was up a few inches higher, and Grandma was going to lie down on the lower one. I tried to give my Papa a kiss, but he wanted to sleep. Outside there was a man named Mike who had dug up my weedy garden box and planted something new. I liked the way it looked. It had fuchsia colored flowers on it.*

At our new house in San Diego, the next door neighbor was Mike. He planted ice plant with fuchsia colored flowers right next to our front yard 11 days before my grandmother passed away on May 9, 1998. I think the image of the beds being at different height levels relates to their place in the spirit world, but not different by much. Obviously I can't know for sure, but I saw the image for a reason. In their lives my grandfather was much more social and quick to want to help friends outside of the family. After my grandma retired from factory work, she really kept just to the family and didn't have many outside friends.

January 26, 1996- *I dreamed I was in a shopping center and I saw a woman with a beautiful dog (it was a sheltie- we got a sheltie – also often called collies in November 96). It was very well trained. We were all in a room together waiting for something. I was playing with the dog. There were irritable feelings between me and the woman owner of the dog. As we were leaving, I saw how well trained the dog was and I knew she must have spent a lot of time with the dog to train it that well. I knew the dog was supposed to have been mine. I had it for a short time as a puppy and she had it from then on. It was like a very surprising revelation.*

This dream is about 2 dogs- the sheltie we got after returning from Okinawa, and a Border Collie my son got later. In March of 2009 my son who was still living at home with me while going to college, bought a puppy Border Collie at a shopping center with his girlfriend. They played with her in a small room before deciding to buy her. He brought her home, and I ended up doing everything for the puppy for several months, she even slept in my bed with me most of the time. I was totally in love with this dog. Then my son moved out and took the dog with him, and ended up giving her to his girlfriend when they broke up. My heart was completely broken. It was a huge shock to me that he would give the dog away. The girlfriend trained her very well, and she is now an expert trick dog and sheep herder. We have stayed in touch and Nikki has given Sam a great life.

May 29, 1996 *I dreamed I was with two men. One of them had given me a gold ring I was wearing and I was turning it on my finger. Then I was at an airport getting ready to go on a trip and there was an emergency and a nurse came into the room and said she had just given a cup of blood for someone who was hurt. I asked her what blood type she was, and she didn't answer me. I said A, B or O? She just said they needed more blood and we had to be donors and she was going to test us. There was something about going somewhere with one of the men I was with on a trip to a faraway country.*

Later that day I got an email from Tony a mutual friend of my high school boyfriend Brian, (later Brian would share that he was gay and had contracted AIDS). Tony said Brian's T-cells were low, but Brian was going to Europe for six weeks anyway. I was equally fascinated and frustrated at how the elements were coming through. They were woven into a complex story with very relevant matching pieces, and yet I was in the story. I think the gold ring was not mine, but one of the men- possibly my former boyfriend and his partner. We had remained friends and he later sent me photos of his boyfriend. Sadly, he passed away shortly after.

Second dream same day

I dreamed I saw my friend Kelly's husband working at a clothing warehouse. I went up the stairs to it and I saw Kelly's name in tattoo style on the door. He had done that for her. On one of the steps was his name in tattoo style as well.

Three days later I went to the beach with Kelly and her husband. I saw they each had tattoos with the other's name. I had never seen her tattoos before.

At the same time I had been keeping my dream journals, I was following The Artist's Way by Julia Cameron and was doing "morning pages". Every morning I was to write three pages regardless of what else was going on, it was advised to write them first thing in the morning. So along with whatever dreams I recalled, I was writing whatever thoughts came into my head in a separate journal. At the time, the pages seemed like gibberish, and I wondered what I would ever do with them. The goal was to allow room for artistic inspiration, but I think I got much more than that.

I often recorded the early morning goings on in my house of the kids waking up and whatever they were saying or asking for, and what my husband was doing in helping them get ready for school before he went off to work. He was very patient with me as I was trying to work through some serious depression. I was trying to figure out how I fit into the world with my kids and having no say in where we lived, and anxiety about the foreign place we were at.

There was so much for me to be thankful for, but when you don't feel a connection you want to your spouse, and your world revolves around their career, it can be tough to feel you have any power in your life of your own. You can feel like a reluctant piece of property. I felt like a piece of furniture he really didn't want to have, and he couldn't figure out what to do with me.

BACK TO THE STATES

In August we moved back to San Diego to a new home and new friends. My grandmother was going to be moving in with us. It was well intentioned, but in hindsight was not a good choice, primarily because my husband's heart was not in it, but he agreed to it anyway. I was sad to be leaving Okinawa. Even though it took me a whole year to adjust to being there, it was an amazing place, and we made great friends there.

I knew going back to the states was going to put more pressure on my marriage, we just didn't seem to be able to reach each other, and we would not have the same kind of easy social life in California that we had in Okinawa to buffer things.

I got my grandma situated in the downstairs guest room which had its own bathroom for her. She shipped her bedroom furniture down from Northern California and set up her tv, a little card table and chair. She spent most of the time reading books in her room or watching the news or Jeopardy! Which was her absolute favorite show. She was so well read that she was a whiz at Jeopardy!

Grandma had to wear her oxygen all the time, and if we went out for errands we had to bring a portable unit with us. She hated this. She was so self-conscious about not only looking like she might be an invalid, but also was terrified of having a coughing attack come on in public. Because she might throw up or lose control of her bladder. It was tough. Decades of smoking took their toll. I tried every way I could as a child to get her to stop smoking, but it was just seen as what people do when I was younger. I would be dramatic and sit low on the ground in the kitchen when she cooked dinner and we were visiting, and I would cover my nose because the smoke burned my nose. It made no difference.

So it was hard later on to see her hooked up to this machine, with those memories of my childhood and my protests that would have likely saved her this indignation and suffering. Addiction to smoking was not considered as serious back then as it is today.

December 27, 1996

I dreamed I was outside a doctor's office waiting to get in. My friend Suzanne was there with me and we were working on something together like a party and it involved getting things together.

January 24, 1997 (almost a month later) I ran into Suzanne at the veterinarian's office. I was there for a check-up with my Sheltie Andy, and she was there with her guinea pig. They both had Mange. She gave me dates for Art Corps meetings where we would learn to teach art to our kids' classes as volunteers. She asked me to bring some beer to the workshop.

THE PRESIDENT

I was surprised to be picking up on news stories. I think I was watching the news now more than I did in Okinawa. Primarily because in Okinawa we only had one channel.

Jan. 11, 1997 *I dreamed I saw President Clinton and three images of him. I saw him lying down injured and he said "I'm not going to run".*

March 15,1997, Clinton fell and required knee surgery to reattach a tendon, and was seen on crutches. (He can't run now)

August 20, 1997- *I dreamed I was at the White House and I saw President Clinton. He and his wife were having problems with their daughter Chelsea. She was in trouble, and Hillary was angry with her and was threatening to take her to jail for a night and she was telling police to come and take her to jail. I don't know what she did that was bad enough to go to jail for. <u>Somebody said she had an</u>*

affair with a married man. Then she was in jail for a day, and she went home and got in bed with mom and dad and the bed seemed crowded.

Same day dream #2- Then I saw President Clinton and he was talking about what he was going to do after his presidency, and he said "I'll be lucky if I have enough energy to change a tire" Which I thought was a very funny expression. He had multiple surgeries: 2004 a coronary bypass, 2005 surgery, and 2010 quadruple bypass surgery.

The Lewinsky affair was brought to light in 1998, and Monica Lewinsky was 22 at the time. She later reported that the FBI threatened her with jail if she did not agree to wear a wire and meet with Clinton, and they denied her a lawyer during her interrogation.

Chelsea was 18 at the time. Lewinsky was young enough to be their daughter. While the dream presented Chelsea as the one in trouble, and clearly she was not the one having an affair, she represented the daughter figure. The bed being "crowded with all three of them" represented the difficult triangle the affair created.

Obviously I don't know, but it could also represent Monica's interrogation as spending a day in jail and then going home to her parents.

I think these were the first famous people I had dreamed about where the elements were relevant even if they weren't a straight linear match. I was more fascinated with the random nature of what I was picking up on without even trying.

Dreams are rarely exactly as they happen, but the elements are relevant, and it's not like I was dreaming about the Clinton's frequently. I think I have less than five dreams about the Clinton's total. Personally, I was a fan of the Clinton's and when I saw everything break on the news I felt badly for them. People make mistakes, we all do at some point in our lives. I know it had nothing to do with whether or not they were good people.

ON THE HOME FRONT

I was not experiencing very frequent hits during this period, approximately one a month.

February 15, 1997 *I dreamed we took (our dog) Andy to the pound to find a playmate for him, and I was outside with him while my husband went inside. I was worried that Andy would think we were going to leave him there.* Later this day my husband went to the pound by himself to look for a dog without telling me beforehand. He was interested in getting a Golden Retriever or a Yellow Lab playmate for Andy. We went back to the pound shortly after and ended up picking out a black lab puppy we named Jasmine.

April 2, 1997 *I dreamed I was visiting my sister in law at a store that was a small wooden house. It looked like unpainted brown wood. It was a gift store.* Her father passed away in January 1999 and she bought a little storefront gallery for her house in Oregon.

June 2, 1997 *I dreamed I was out front in the driveway. I saw my next door neighbor driving a little red Volkswagen bug.* Around 2012 they bought a red Volkswagen beetle for their middle daughter's 16th birthday. It now sits out front every day while she is away at college. I only discovered this dream in March of 2015.

June 6, 1997 I was wakened in the middle of the night by a vibration like a cat purring on my legs with no weight to it. I felt it was my beautiful 16 year old calico cat Huggy who had died a week to the day earlier, and she was doing her regular routine with me of going under my sheets to my feet and then back up. I remained awake and felt a lot of love toward Huggy. I lifted the sheets and whispered her name in hopes of seeing her, but I did not. She remained there and moved around a bit for several minutes. I felt very comforted by the experience. I missed her a lot.

A PRAYER FOR DIANA

August 31, 1997 Princess Diana died. I was devastated. We were the same age and I had been a big fan of hers. Sept. 1, I wanted to pray for her, but I didn't know if I could do it. I had cried too much.

I got out my rosary that my grandmother had given me when I was little and took it to bed to help. Around 11:35 I was awakened by something, and I saw a white square hanging over the bed. It was over my husband and me. It was three feet wide and maybe a foot thick. It was intangible and looked like white cloud material, but opaque. There were no openings that I could see through.

I was shocked at what I saw and I sat up straight in bed awake, I gasped out loud. I had no idea what it was, or why I was seeing it. There seemed to be significance to the time. It was either 11:35 or 11:53 but I felt for some reason I was supposed to see what time it was. I had never heard of anything like it before.

I wondered was it from some kind of collective grief energy, or just my own. Was it sent to observe me? Or just to acknowledge that I was grieving Princess Diana. But why a box, what the heck was it? One day I hope to have it figured out, but I may never know.

September 20, 1997- *I dreamed I was going downstairs to the garage to see the Nintendo video game my son had left on the counter the day before.* Then I woke up to find my son sitting by the bed next to me on the floor, silently waiting for me to wake up so he could ask me if he could turn off the house alarm and go in the garage to get the Nintendo game. There were multiple times where my son's thoughts or actions have entered my dreams when he was still living at home. I think they were evidence of the deep connection we shared. Since he moved out on his own I rarely dream about him. I kind of miss it.

August 14, 1997 I had a confusing dream about one of the doctors we had known in Okinawa, that we got a call Chris was dead of a heart attack. In the morning I thought my husband had been on the phone, and I jumped to conclusions and said out loud "Chris is dead". He said, I wasn't on the phone, what are you talking about? Then in October *I dreamed I was at a wedding that I was not invited to, it was as if I had stumbled onto it and it involved my friend from Okinawa Michelle/. I noted that something was odd or different about the wedding.*

Michelle's husband died on Father's Day 1998 of a heart attack, and he was best friends with Chris who went to the funeral and I was so distraught I basically invited myself to the funeral. What was "odd" was that it was a funeral, not a wedding. This was very sudden without warning, and we were the same age. It was a huge shock, and my heart was broken for his family. Later I had a dream that I thought was Rick giving me a message for Michelle, but I wasn't able to catch the message, and there was no second attempt.

Sadly, Rick's dad passed suddenly a couple of weeks later as well. April 16, 1998 (a couple of months before they passed) *I dreamed my husband told me a friend had died of a heart attack at the hospital* (he was a doctor and died at work at the hospital), *and they couldn't save him. There was something about an airplane and a woman learning to fly, a group of women and my friends Karin and Lisa were there.* The night before the funeral at my hotel in San Jose my friends Karin and Lisa came to visit me. I met a friend of Michelle's who was a woman pilot, at the funeral.

October 16, 1997-When I was falling asleep I heard a female's voice in my right ear. It startled me and I looked around, but I didn't see anyone and I wondered if I had made that noise while I was sleeping, but it didn't sound like me. I had been asking to meet my guides, so I was hopeful it was related to that.

While I was waking up in the morning I saw part of a painting with a large leaf on it. It was lightly painted green and looked smooth and soft and beautiful. I wished I could paint that well. I wrote "I can only hope it's a painting of mine in the future". Before my alarm went off I had a sensation that my back felt light, as if something was urging me to leave my body, but I couldn't figure out how to do it. I tried to visualize myself getting up and walking around the bed and felt like it could almost happen, yet I did feel some fear of it too. I'd read in Elisabeth Kubler-Ross' book "The Wheel of Life" how to try to do it. (Astral projection)

October 17, 1997 *I dreamed that we had just moved to a new place, and my husband started rearranging furniture, and then I saw that he was taking his dresser which was full of clothes and he was taking it away somewhere as if he was moving out.* He ended up moving out in February 2000. While this was something that at times seemed almost inevitable due to our lack of ability to connect, there was a sense that he had no desire to connect anymore. I never stopped loving him, we just could not figure out how to click with each other, and life was too short to keep on living the way we were together if there was not going to be significant effort to fix things. In the end, I think he was much happier after all, in his new life and I wish him all the best.

FAMILY DEATHS

November 9 1997. I dreamed about my grandmother, (who had been living with us for a year at this point), and was quite depressed about her life, rarely came out of her room, and I think really just wanted to die. *I dreamed she moved to China. It was a foreign country and she didn't speak the language. She found herself an apartment. Her landlord lived in the same building. It was more like a house, and he lived in a part that was attached to it. He was Chinese and did not speak English. It was an old place. The linoleum was cracking and curling up. I was surprised that she got the place herself. My Aunt tried to call her, but could not get through. She and my uncle flew out to see her and I talked to them. I was there with Grandma at her place. She was telling me things I needed to do for her. I felt like a slave.*

Later that day my Grandma told me a story about taking care of her brother's money for him while he was away during the war. She sent it to him by ship, but the ship sank and he never got it. He accused her of using the money for herself and she said "that idea was so foreign to me". Six months later after she came home from the hospital she was telling me to get her this or that "where's my watch? As in "get it for me now". I had become a full time caregiver for her. Which I was ok with, but the stress was more that my husband was unhappy with my grandmother living with us. She passed away on my birthday at my home on May 9th , with my aunt and I by her side. We had talked a few times about life after death, and being a devout Catholic she was planning to see my Papa again in Heaven. Since she had told me about seeing her mother after she passed away, I asked her if she could try to come see me sometime after she died. She said she would try, but it wasn't a favorite topic of discussion for her. I was wanting more proof, and she told me I was too persistent.

The night that she passed away, I told her "you are going on my birthday", and she nodded her head. I know it was a meaningful date to her. She always made me feel special when I was little. It was hard to see her life get to a place where she felt she had nothing more to live for. Her mind was as sharp as a tack and she could give any Jeopardy! contestant a run for their money while watching it nightly at home, and she read voraciously, sometimes 5 books a week. But her body was not cooperating anymore. She was 84.

The horrible coughing from Emphysema wore her down in many ways, not only the pain in her chest and throat, but also the potential social embarrassment if we were out in public and a coughing spell would hit her. Reluctantly I agreed to respect her decision to not take antibiotics for her bronchitis. She managed to visit me after she passed away, but it wasn't anything like I had imagined.

My youngest brother James died of an accidental alcohol valium mix at Thanksgiving 1998. I had a couple of dreams prior to that which seemed to be relevant to his unexpected and tragic death.

November 14, 1997- *I was at a house where a robber came in and I was trying to call 911. The guy looked like my brother James. And then our dad was there. I felt a lot of frustration and I didn't want to be around that situation at all.* He was found unconscious in a house with friends late at night. They called 911, but the house was hard to find and he was brain dead by the time the ambulance reached him.

July 20, 1998 (two months after my grandmother passed away) *I dreamed I was in a room like Grandma's old room, though it looked different from her room here. It seemed like it was the room she died in. She looked younger and she wasn't heavy looking anymore. She was wearing a creamy silky colored outfit. I couldn't believe it. She looked totally real to me. I hugged her tightly and told her I loved her. She told me she loved me too. Papa was also in the room sitting down on a chair next to the tv. Grandma said something about "now that I'm dead", and I knew it was really her spirit I was talking to. She came to tell me something but she didn't seem comfortable telling me the details. She said Tuesday the 27th or 29th, and I wanted to know what was going to happen. She left the room with my Papa, and a man came in to help me. He was going to fix me a cappuccino.*

There were two tvs in the room side by side. I told him what Grandma had said, and he looked surprised and said she wasn't supposed to tell me anything. This only increased my concern that it must be something serious, and I had to know. I told him she didn't tell me what was supposed to happen, and I asked him to show me pictures on the tvs. I was pushy and very serious. I pointed at the tv and I repeated "please show me!" I knew he knew what was going to happen. He asked me to follow him. We went outside to a factory warehouse looking kind of building. There was a back entrance with a narrow dark opening at the ground he wanted me climb down into. There was a metal slide with spikey shapes that would cut you if you went down. I asked him to go first. I was not about to go down there. Clearly it was going to be painful and scary. Then I woke up.

The dream was only 2 and a half months since my grandma had passed away, and here she was already trying to tell me something she wasn't allowed to tell me. I was happy to see her, but I was very frustrated that she didn't tell me what they came to tell me.

When I got the call from my brother's employer (the day after Thanksgiving, November 27th) that he was in the hospital, and it was very serious and we better come now, I called the rest of my family and we all flew separately from different locations to Seattle. I arrived first, and James' employers were kind enough to pick me up at the airport. In the ICU, James was on life support hooked up to a breathing machine, unconscious and swollen from edema. It was very unreal. He was only 27, he was a kid. My baby brother. I didn't want to believe the diagnosis of brain death. How could that be? It had to be wrong. It couldn't be possible. While I waited for my parents and two other brothers to arrive, I stood by his bed, holding his hand.

When he was little and only 16 months old, he had climbed on top of the air conditioning unit in our back yard in Virginia. He had fallen and split his head open, and my mother and I drove him to the hospital.

I had to hold a towel to his head to stop the bleeding on the ride to the hospital. He got stitches on his forehead and was hospitalized for about a week. I was eleven years older than him, and that event solidified my protective feelings for him after that. I couldn't believe we were going to have to say goodbye, and yet at the same time, it had been a fear we all had for some time.

Two of his friends who were quite edgy, grungy, almost creepy and his partners in crime I guess, arrived and wanted to visit him. I felt very nervous around them and I wasn't sure of their motive, but I allowed them to come in for a few minutes. I partly blamed them for being part of that *living dangerously* life with him. While we stood there, the guys were talking somewhat crudely about what James might be able to do in the after-life, as if he was already dead.

The big pendant light over his bed in the ICU started to flicker on and off with a zap sound and even seemed to move a bit. Something definitely happened in response to what the guys were saying. We all noticed it, and they got so freaked out by it they left. Maybe that was the point. This was a sacred time with James, during our last few hours with him, and those guys didn't need to be there anymore. Whether it was my brother, or something else that made the light flicker that way I can't know for sure, but it seemed like James was really there with us.

My brother had a donor card in his wallet, and we made the heart wrenching decision to donate his organs. This was excruciatingly difficult, the most horrible situation to be in, because his body was still alive.

I wanted a miracle more than anything. But the doctors told us it wasn't possible. Our hearts were completely ripped open. We were all crying. My mother and I each put lipstick on and kissed him all over his face, covering his face with kiss marks before we had to say goodbye for the last time. It was unbearable. I learned later that he was able to save the lives of three people from his donations.

After we said our final goodbyes to him, we stopped by the apartment where he had been staying to collect his things. A small studio apartment he shared with a woman. The front room was almost exactly the same as the room where my Grandma and Papa had been when my Grandma was trying to tell me some news.

I realized **that** was how she was trying to tell me, without giving it away. I'm sure they knew I would have tried to save him if she told me, and for whatever reason, it was not my place to do that. James' employers told me that James had planned to surprise me and come down for a visit with me at Christmas. To this day that is the one thing that I cannot think of without being overcome by emotion.

Shortly after, I went to meet James' two year old daughter Malone in Los Angeles. She was a virtual clone of him. I could not believe it. She had the exact same face and expressions. I had never seen a child look so identical to their parent before. It was spooky and miraculous at the same time. A big part of him lives on in her.

NEW SPIRITUAL COMMUNITY

January 18, 1998 was my first day attending the Church of Today, a non-denominational Unity church. I had met the minister Wendy who happened to live in my neighborhood, we all kind of moved into the neighborhood at the same time because it was a new development.

I dreamed I saw the waterfall wall ripped away from the wall with plasterboard underneath. It was being renovated. But at church the water wall was in perfect condition, and I made a note of confusion about this in my journal. I quickly became involved in the church, volunteering in the office, the Sunday school, and even joined the prayer partner group to offer prayer support to other church members. After the end of my marriage, I felt very disillusioned with prayer for a time, and by 2002 I stopped going to church altogether.

In May 2015, after being reignited by this whole

book project that had come to life in March, I decided to go to church again, as I reopened the spiritual side of my life. At my first visit back to the church now called The Unity Center, I saw the water wall was under renovation with a scaffolding. It was being repainted and a new look was underway. I only found the dream after doing another review to prepare for this book. There may yet be dreams still to come true, waiting to be discovered or actualized.

The waking "sightings" were always random and unexpected. Regardless of how tame the image appeared to be, it always startled me into grabbing my husband. Thankfully with one exception they have only happened when I was not alone.

March 1, 1998- I woke up early in the morning around 1 am. I looked over at my husband and felt a presence next to him (I doubt a hypnogogic hallucination can include a sensation of someone being in the room with you as this felt). I saw a white shape that may have had a design on it. Possibly some kind of scrollwork at the top. I thought the shape resembled a tombstone, but I thought it looked like an official document and it was thick. I gasped out loud, as I usually did at seeing anything out of place during the night, and my husband grasped my arm and tried to comfort me, then it disappeared. My husband did not remember in the morning waking up to grab my arm.

I remember that these kind of events, while completely mysterious and mystical left me feeling like I was being watched by forces on another plane, or they were possibly meant to energize my spiritual questioning, but in any event, I felt like I was completely failing at understanding them. I did note that again, the time was before 3 am, which seemed to be the case for anything that was apparently more spiritual in nature.

March 22, 1998- *I dreamed about being at a beach resort with my son and daughter, and we saw leopard sharks in the water.* Later that day, my son and I were at a store shopping for a birthday gift for his friend Ben. My son picked up a leopard shark, and I said that was just like in my dream.

Things like this happened all the time in short term dream precognition events. They happened the most with my son, and without prompting he would do or say something that was clearly related to the dream from that morning. I would guess it relates to the level of connection that we shared, though I was picking up on trivial events involving my friends as well.

MEETING A GUIDE

March 27, 1998- After going to my first Course in Miracles class, *I dreamed that I heard the voice of one of my guides as if she was talking to me clearly. I saw her face, and I was shown a photo of her as a nun at a convent or place that Mother Teresa had lived at or built, possibly one of her missions. She was in the middle of two other nuns in the Polaroid photo. I think her name was Debbie.* As if to give me proof that she was real, she tickled the bottom of my right foot two times and I woke up and looked around but did not see her.

I went back to sleep and the dream continued a little bit. It looked like my Papa lived at the same place she did and I saw him briefly. I think my Grandma was there too. Maybe Debbie was originally from Pennsylvania like my grandparents were. I was not able to remember more of what she said to me. At that time she looked older than me. She was in her 40s or 50s.

April 9, 1998- *I dreamed I was writing in my journal book and the voice of God was talking to me and I was writing His words. When I read the words I had written, I realized what was going on, and it said something like "This is the book of God", and it went longer than that, but I can't remember what it said. My reaction was NO, I'm not ready to do this (write a book for God), and God was telling me yes, I was.* Well, that certainly had me puzzled. How can you dream about that and NOT remember what it was that "God" had said? And who says NO to God? I think maybe I didn't believe it was really God in the dream. But while I was skeptical of this dream being what it was supposed to be, I was not wanting to write it off completely. Though at the time of this writing, nothing definitive has emerged (that I am aware of) to make this dream a reality so far. I have included it mostly because I hadn't remembered having a dream like this, and part of me is holding out for something more to develop down the road. It can happen right?

There was another unusual dream April 12, 1998- *I was with a group of people who were being chosen for something. We were in a building with chairs and it curved around a wall area. I saw Oprah Winfrey in there with the group as we waited for something big to happen, and more people kept coming. We were all in a single file line. I started getting a closed in feeling and a woman said to me*

"Time is waking up", and I had the idea that was who was coming- Time, and I wondered what that meant. This one has not played out as far as I know, but I am intrigued by the idea that "Time is coming" or "Time is waking up". The time is coming....

August 8, 1995: *I dreamed I was with my mother in law (who had died in April). She was wearing a navy blue dress and she looked pretty. I went and gave her a hug, and told her how much I had missed her, and I think I was starting to cry. She said "really?" Then she said "I bought you a ticket home for your birthday". I said where? She said "Florida". I was surprised that she considered Florida my home. I was confused but knew my aunt and uncle lived there, so I supposed it could be home. There was a little girl that was a relative of hers who was showing her a certificate of some kind from school, and Beverly leaned over to kiss it. She said she is around when nobody knows.* A ticket home for my birthday. It was confusing.

My grandma died on my birthday- she got her ticket "home". But the year before we went to Hawaii for my birthday- where I had lived as a kid. I didn't know what to think.

We had a tough relationship when she was alive. I don't think she wanted me for her son, though she tried to be generous with me, it was always infused with her disapproval. On my birthday the month after her death I was walking down the hall in our house in Okinawa and I walked through a spot in the hallway that had the exact smell of her kitchen at the family home in Marin. I stopped and stood there for a minute and took it in. I said hi Bev. I wished I could hear a response. I wished the rest of her family could know she was reaching out. Not to mention the meaning it could have had for my husband if he was open to it. I felt this was her way of saying happy birthday.

January 5, 1996 I dreamed I was in California and I found out that my former boyfriend had been visiting Concord (where we graduated high school). He had been there twice and didn't tell me. I was disappointed to have been close by and missed seeing him. January 11, I got an email from our mutual friend that he had been in Concord and he had missed a chance to see him. I called him and was told he was in Concord the day before to see Brian (who was my high school boyfriend and their mutual friend).

February 16, 1996 One of my girlfriends in Okinawa was very very dear and generous, but we got caught up in an awkward social triangle and some jealousy and misunderstandings which caused me to back off from our interactions. She had seemed to go overboard on giving, and I didn't know how to receive it.

I dreamed my friend was at my house. Her arms were full of wrapped gift boxes, and I was trying to figure out who they were for. They were for a birthday, and it felt very awkward, I felt like it highlighted the difficulty in our relationship. In May she came over for my birthday and she brought 6 or 8 gifts for me. We would be moving back to the states in August and it was like she was giving me all the gifts she had saved up for me. Nobody had ever given me so many gifts before. In a way it was heart breaking, like we were meant to be sisters, but our paths just did not allow for that.

My grandma died at my home on my birthday at 4 am May 9, 1998. We had planned to go on vacation, but she got sick and she went in the hospital with bronchitis. After a couple of days in the hospital she wanted to come home. Her doctor told her that if she went home she was not going to survive. She said it was ok, she didn't care. I think she was ready to go. Her first night home she seemed to go into in a coma and my husband told me he didn't think she would make it through the night, but I stayed with her. We had hospice set her up with a catheter, and they brought a suction machine which I had to use. She woke up in the middle of the night and called me into her room and said "I want a banana milkshake". She had never asked me for a milkshake before. So I made one.

My aunt and uncle flew out to be with us from Florida. At midnight on my birthday she called me down to her room and said she just wanted me there. I think she knew it was coming soon. I couldn't believe it. She passed four hours later.

My mom flew out to be with us for a while May 19, 1998. She missed saying goodbye to her mother. They had not seen each other in twenty years. They had a horrible fight on Thanksgiving of 1978, and they never spoke again. I think the black fog from when I was young was possibly related to their estrangement. *I dreamed I saw my mom holding a piece of paper and she was telling me something about the date on it.* Later that day she came out of my grandma's room with her death certificate, and she showed me they had put the wrong date for her death on the certificate.

April 10, 1997- *Just as I was falling asleep around 11:30 I dreamed, but* ***it felt completely real****, that I was rising up and was surrounded by nothing but whiteness all around me (even though it was dark in my room). As I went up, the atmosphere got progressively whiter and whiter, and when I stopped ascending, a man's voice spoke to me, but I saw no one. I sensed what direction he was in, and I turned and faced him to my right. He said "What is your name and why have you come?" I answered that I wanted help with my clairvoyance, and to see more clearly. Boom!*

Immediately, I was awake and back in my bed.

Startled is an understatement. In a way I think I felt like a kid who had gotten in the wrong line for a special event and got sent back to the end of the line. Where did I go? How did that happen? Who was the man, and why didn't he know who I was? I guess I had a chance to make my intentions known, and I hoped that whoever I had spoken to would get my message to the right place. I was thinking I needed external help to make this happen for me, but now I see that there was more work that I had to do on my own as well. You can't just levitate up into heaven and expect to be all seeing when you come back.

Yet somehow I managed to get to that place. This happened to be on my husband's birthday. What if it was actually a near death experience? Could I have almost died? I wasn't sick, I didn't feel like anything was wrong with me, it just spontaneously happened.

But I have come to believe that there are few accidents if any in these type of things. So there must have been a reason. When I think of why I didn't get some kind of verbal response, my mind wants to compare it to a judge who can't be bothered with a long explanation and just calls out "next case". Clearly I didn't have enough together yet. But there was value in even that little bit of experience, because obviously I'm writing about it right now.

May 10, 1997- *I dreamed someone was coming to my house and he had a big dog that looked like a Mastiff. I was overwhelmed with its size and strength and felt a sense of fear about the dog. Dream #2 -there was some kind of appliance at our house that wasn't working and someone came to fix it. He was the one with the dog I was afraid of.*

September 2011 I met a guy who wanted to date me who was a remodeling contractor. He had a Mastiff. I did feel a sense of a Mastiff being an overwhelming sized dog. It was clear we were not going to be a match, but I allowed him to offer a quote when I was contemplating renovating my kitchen in May 2012. After my first quote from another company came in much higher than I had even considered, I gave the job to the guy with the Mastiff. My new kitchen got underway. I got a whole new kitchen and appliances. I thought it was interesting that the dreams were on the same day, yet split, just like the way I met the guy, and first heard all about his dog who was like his kid, and then another dream, where he came to work on the house. Two separate dreams of related events on the same day, which played out eight months apart fourteen years later!

August 10, 1997 (I notice a pattern of things happening on the 10th) *I dreamed a big disaster was going to happen, either a fire or a storm was going to come to the big building that looked like a warehouse, and we were trying to get out before it came. I ended up at a woman's house. She had kids and a baby sleeping. My daughter was interested in some of the toys they had there. I took some girl toys like dolls. It was as if some of the things were from Okinawa. I was going downstairs with them and trying not to wake up the baby. I saw a yellow quilt, the lady of the house did sewing.*

October 2003, we got evacuation notice in my neighborhood of Scripps Ranch from the Cedar fire. By then I was divorced and my husband had remarried. Their home was about 10 minutes away in an area that was out of range of the fires. I packed my kids up and took them to my ex-husband's house. His wife offered for all of us to stay there, but I just dropped my kids off and returned home. His second wife is a quilter, and in their first Christmas together she quilted a table runner as a gift to me, which was quite generous and kind. My ex-husband frequently worked nights and had to sleep in the day time; hence not wanting to wake the baby.

October 12, 1998 -This was a very unusual experience for a couple of reasons. Number one, my husband rarely remembered his dreams, in the entire time I had known him (18 years at this point), he probably shared less than 5 dream recalls with me. I rarely caught him in the act of dreaming, but to have dreams with a common theme and same time period on the same day, that was something I never expected... Was this a past life memory? A tandem dream?

My dream: *I dreamed I was at a castle. I was a man. I was a knight and I had just returned from a trip and I brought a gold pin for the king. (Although he looked different, I knew he was my current husband). The pin was a flat pin with a shape of a human form wearing heavy clothes. I gave it to the king. He was Caucasian with the same color hair and same age he was at the time of the dream (39 yrs.). He took a knife and pushed it into my heart. I felt the blade enter my body. I fell to the ground and lay there with the knife in my chest, knowing I was going to die, and not knowing why the man did that to me. I was stunned and I was waiting to take my last breath. I could feel my chest stopping the act of breathing. It was an intense feeling of pressure on my chest where the knife was, and I kept thinking why? Why? Why? Why did he do this?*

In the morning I saw him still asleep and he had been bouncing in bed. I knew something violent was going on.

His dream: *He said he was a castle guard, and he saw an Asian man kill another guard. He knew the man was there to kill everyone and he was afraid for his life, so he killed the man first by decapitating him. Afterwards he was talking to someone else about it and he said he used a sword and he had to use it sideways to avoid it collapsing on itself. He was afraid of getting stabbed. We both had castle dreams about someone being killed with a blade. In my dream he killed someone- me.*

December 28, 1998- *I dreamed about my husband's parents. They were both there. It had something to do with their giving away their belongings to all their kids.* Jan. 11, 1999 my husband's father passed away. January 25, 1999 - *I dreamed I was with my husband and his brother and sisters at their dad's house. Their dad was there. He looked well and like his usual self. He was talking to all of us as a group about his investments and he said "they were just investments", and he said we should all put the money away in savings and it was important to him that we do it.* I could feel that my father in law was trying to watch out for us.

March 9, 1999 - *I dreamed I saw my old boyfriend writing me a letter telling me his mother died two months ago. He put lots of papers in with it and I started to read them. It looked like he had made a will for himself. I also saw him shopping for a ring for his wife.* He confirmed he had bought a sapphire for her that she put into a ring. March 31, I talked to him. His mom died Jan. 18, 1999.

May 7, 1999 *I dreamed I was dating a man who was 70 years old but he looked 30. He was asking if I could be interested in him. I said "you've already decided you want to be with me?"* February 2013 I met a handsome dentist who was 67. He showed me a photo in a yearbook from one of the ships he was on in the Navy of himself at age 30, and he looked like Richard Gere. I was stunned. I told him it would have been love at first sight if I met him then. He very quickly decided he wanted to get serious with me within a couple of weeks of dating, and was showing me a room I could keep my things in, but I was concerned about the age gap, and I didn't think I could do it. I cared for him very much, he was very generous and caring to his patients, but there were too many other things not in alignment with us. This dream was 13 years before the event. I have no idea why they have come at different periods of time, other than for this one, at this particular period in my life I was desperately wanting a healthy love relationship. My marriage was ending, there was great emotional turmoil in my waking life, and so maybe in my sleep I went out to the future and got a peek at one that would be coming into my life. Even though that relationship did not work out, I greatly value having met and spent time with him.

Lucid Dreams- This is a very special state of sleep where even though you are sleeping, you are also totally awake. You know it's a dream, and whether you are navigating through a dream landscape or scenario, or whether you are navigating through the earthly plane, you have complete control of your actions if you choose to, and basically have super powers that allow you to breathe under water, swim, fly and test your creativity for creating activities and scenes for you to navigate through, almost like your own personal video game.

There are many books on this subject, and I would encourage you to check them out if you would like to try lucid dreaming for yourself. This is one type of dream that is possibly the most exhilarating you can ever have. It feels real, and you experience physical sensations as you might expect to under similar conditions in the waking world.

My first lucid dream! August 27, 1999 *I was in the ocean with some other people and there was a large ocean animal nearby. We were floating on the surface and the animal was submerged enough that I could not tell whether it was a shark or a dolphin. I wanted to get out of there just in case it was a shark. I popped up and then realized I had* *control of my actions and wanted to move in the water like a dolphin and then I came out of the water into the air, and soared way up and came down over a city. It was like a ride at Disneyland and it was at night. I hovered above the city and tried to reach my hand down to touch the city as if it was a model of city buildings. I don't know what city it was, but it was big. I was having so much fun. It was like being on a roller coaster but I had control of where and when I went.* When I woke up I realized it had been lucid, and I was so disappointed it was over. I tried to go back to sleep and have it continue, but it didn't. It was the most fun I had ever had in a dream.

In the early stages of writing this book, I was doing intensive reviews of the dream journals, and frequently I would find myself feeling disappointed. With so many dreams that came true, why didn't I dream about certain people who have come and gone in my life. Why would I dream about some people by *name* before I met them, who really didn't stay connected to me, and others who were emotionally more of a big deal to me, seemingly escaped without anything. And then I was reading a dream that I know I must have reviewed before, and suddenly it became clear that I had missed something.

May 3, 2000 This is one of those dreams that I don't feel great about sharing because it puts someone in a bad light, and it remains an emotionally charged issue, but I feel the circumstance is interesting enough, and it was fairly dramatic at the time, I have decided to include it. And in the process of writing even this section, I discovered a dream 6 years earlier about a different part of the same event, and that dream was 9 years before the event, and 7 years before I met the guy involved. So I have two dreams now to decipher.

This all involved a summer road trip (about 2 years after my divorce) in August of 2002 with my two kids and a complicated new relationship. We first drove to Zion National Park for a few days and saw the Grand Canyon.

While at Zion, we hiked and walked through a river in a slot canyon we were in awe of the place, it was in many ways like being in another world, and for some time my daughter was happily carried on the back of my friend, who was using a hiking stick.

Then on the way home the decision was made to stop at Disneyland for my daughter's birthday, which was that day. Here is the first dream: January 14, 1994- *Dreamed I was at Disneyland with my family. There was a weird attraction that had poles with a foot support on either side and you had to hold on and step up to the next part and there was some kind of rule to it. There was a young girl hanging on to my back. Not sure if it was Kayla, more like an older girl* (Kayla was only 3 at the time of the dream- she was 12 at the time of the event). *I had a sense of competition that I could do this with an extra weight on my back. It was hard, but I could still do it. There was a guy who was in charge of the attraction who had dark hair who was watching, and there was a young woman at the next level who was encouraging people to come up.*

I see in this dream I was in Gary's place in terms of carrying my daughter on his back. And I think he wanted to impress us that he could do it. I see the description as more telling than the visual from the dream. "There was a guy who was in charge of the attraction who had dark hair" In this situation, he had planned the trip and he was definitely in charge of the "attraction". As I wrote it I was unaware of the real meaning of the "attraction", not only of the place, but our relationship as well. And the sticks, even though the dream made them look like stilts, the description fits with hiking and using them to support your feet and step up. He found the walking stick himself. And yes he had dark hair.

These dreams are far from literal, but when you see the combined elements and description itself tells more than the visual did, you can see how you have to really pay attention when reviewing dreams. And when you commit to doing your best to write an honest description, you will have to trust that what you choose to write is as it should be, and will tell you more than you realized when you read it back. When I first began reviewing dreams, I focused more on the visual I remembered, rather than the written description, but it can be either or, they can both have their own way of telling you what happened.

The second dream pertains more to the Disneyland part of the trip: May 3, 2000 *I dreamed I was at an amusement park, but first I was at some other place. An investigation was going on, and some other people were trying to conceal the information we were seeking. At the amusement park I was with a man and some children. I was not sure who the man was. He had a bag of gifts he wanted to find a place to get them wrapped. While he went on rides with the kids I took the gifts to get them wrapped. I got directions to one of the wrapping stations but I couldn't find it. So I went back down to the main outside level and looked for another place there. I couldn't find the man and it was time to leave. The kids were with me. I saw I had different things in my hands than what had been given to me. I thought somehow we would meet up and all be together again.*

In 2001 I started dating a guy who was not right for me, but for a number of reasons I wasn't able to let it go as I should have. The connection was too strong, but it would just be one disappointment after another. In 2002 we took a trip to Zion and the Grand Canyon with my two kids (12 and 14 at the time) where we all had a great time, on the way home we decided to stop at Disneyland for the day on my daughter's 12th birthday in August.

The day started out well, although Gary was complaining about the overly cheerful staff at the park- he hated Disneyland (which was a bit of a red flag) and the kids and I decided to go on some rollercoaster rides, but Gary did not want to come with us on those rides, so he was going to sit on a bench nearby and wait for us. The line for the first ride at Splash Mountain was fairly long, but as soon as we got off the ride, we went to the bench to get Gary. No Gary. Maybe he went to the men's room... so we waited, and waited, for 20 minutes. No Gary.

Ok, well this was Kayla's birthday, and I wasn't going to ruin it waiting for him all day. So we proceeded to the next ride. Periodically we checked back at that same bench all day long, which became an increasing irritation. We were all disappointed. After Pirates of the Carribean, still no luck. We did not have cell phones with us or we could have called him. By the end of the night, after the fireworks there was no sign of him. We waited in the car for nearly an hour after the park closed. No Gary. So we drove home to San Diego without him.

Later I learned he had been at the lost and found office all day expecting us come by, but by 8pm he went to a hotel. I suppose lost and found might have been a reasonable place to look for him (if he was a kid), but I had such a strong feeling that his refusal to go on rides on my daughter's birthday was such a selfish thing to do, I was not going to look for him anywhere but the last place he had been. Really it was just a big red flashing sign that I was not supposed to be with this person. It was a moment of opportunity to see that.

So in the dream where it says first I was at *some other place*- we were at Zion before going to the amusement park. The bag of gifts must have been the marker to my daughter's birthday. Looking for the different wrapping stations, relates to our continuing to check back at the bench where we last saw him. Frequently in dreams I take the place of other people, so while it says the man went on some rides with the kids- I often switch places with people I dream about, and I am them and they are me. So maybe he went off to find a gift for my daughter's birthday, but due to the stress of the rest of the day and how it all turned out we never got that piece of information. *I saw I had different things in my hands than what had been given to me.* There were no gifts after all, and he was not who I had thought he was. We shouldn't have had to go looking for him at lost and found. We had checked that bench more than a dozen times throughout the day. If I had let this relationship go at this point in time, things would have been very different.

I see an interesting and yet frustrating point to these dreams, they are clouded many times in a way that prevents me from seeing the warning they could be, and in hindsight after reviewing it, enough pieces were there to make it a match. So while they were not helpful to me in terms of alerting me to avoid some choices I might make, they illustrate that I was picking up on them well before the event, and at times, even before meeting the person involved. Why could my dream state not help me out more in navigating away from potential trouble coming toward me? I do remember that I had a gut feeling at the time, along with some common sense which I didn't follow. Years later I have resolved to be a better listener to my still small voice in these things. I highly recommend it.

Waking premonition: When my daughter was 16, one day I was dropping her off at the house of a male friend whom I had never met. I think some of their friends were getting together there. It was my first time meeting him (and my last). Something moved inside me with a funny feeling about him and I told her to *never get into a car with that boy.* I never said that to her about anyone else after that. It wasn't until two years later that she finally confided in me that shortly after I met that boy and told her to not get in a car with him, that during a weekend at her dad's she had a date with that same boy.

He picked her up in his dad's convertible, and was showing off the on the road. He lost control of the car, it FLIPPED over and went down a hill off the road! They had to be helped out of the car by passersby and, miraculously there was not a scratch on her. Words cannot express my shock that nobody told me about the accident at the time it happened, but that's a whole other story.

CURRENT TIME

In March 2015 I began recording my dreams again. On the first entry there was a "hit".

March 14, 2015- *I dreamed I was in a house with my mother. There was no furniture. A kitchen sink was in the corner against the wall and the drain was open. It had no hardware or disposal installed and the hole was so large a sponge could fall down into it.*

At the first week of April my mother discovered a lot of water damage in her flooring, and when a repairman came to check it out, a discovery was made that the damage was the result of a plumbing leak that had been going on for some time. She had to move out of her house to a hotel for three months while the floors and some walls were ripped out and replaced. All of her furniture had to be moved and stored in one of the bedrooms and out onto her carport where it sat for three months during the repairs. This was my first dream recorded since starting back into journaling after my 13 year break.

March 19, 2015- *Dreamed I was being told again that I would be able to help people with these spiritual or psychic things I was doing one day soon. I wanted to know when.*

With revisiting all of these experiences, the big thing that has come up for me has been well, obviously there is receptivity happening for events that have not yet happened, but they are random and happen at night when I'm asleep, and for the most part have seemed to be trivial. I am more interested now in having information come that is useful and can help people.

March 27, 2015 I dreamed two times that my photographer friend Charlene was in a car crash with a drunk driver and someone did not survive. I was told Charlene was going to die on April first. This was with no images and just a voice I heard. I heard "Charlene is going to die in a car crash with a DUI driver on April 1st. I woke up and I was stunned. If I had been someone who had not had an extensive number of dreams come true previous to this, it would have been easier to brush off. But it was crystal clear, and it repeated itself.

This was the first time I had gotten a message for someone else. I had not seen Charlene in a few months, but just the day before a mutual friend of ours mentioned that she had given Charlene a referral for a photo shoot, and then Charlene contacted me asking to borrow some photography props for a newborn shoot she had coming up. I had just had the dream and I didn't know what to do. Should I say something? Should I not? Wow.

I was really stumped. I did some meditation to think about it, and I made the decision to go ahead and mention it to her, but very carefully. She was coming by to pick up the props, and I decided to talk to her about it then. This was just three days before the first of April. I had done some thinking about it, and I realized that her ex-husband had been an alcoholic (they divorced since I had known her), and things were not always crystal clear- it didn't necessarily mean SHE would die, but maybe someone close to her, so that maybe "part of her" would die.

I just knew that I have rarely gotten things exactly as you would expect them to be. But I felt like it was worth looking like an idiot if it made her more careful on April 1st. Though I did worry she might think it was the strangest scariest April Fool's joke anyone had ever done on her too. So she arrived and we sorted through the props that she was interested in borrowing, and then I asked her if she had a couple of minutes, and could she sit down with me on the couch. I gave a brief overview of my past history with psychic intuition and dreams, and told her what had recently happened to cause me to start keeping dream journals again.

Then I said, well I had an interesting dream about you a couple of days ago, and it repeated to me two times, so I feel it's worth saying something to you. I hope it's wrong, but I think you should take extra care on the road on April 1st just in case. I dreamed that something serious could happen, and I just wanted to let you know so you can take caution on the road. Her eyes were wide, and I could tell it probably scared her a bit and I hadn't even told her that I was told she was going to die. I didn't see any point in telling her that part.

I told her I had never gotten a message like that for someone before, and I didn't know what to think of it yet, but I was wanting to put it out there for her just in case. I worried it would freak her out and she might never speak to me again. She got up to go with the props she was borrowing and thanked me. She left with a very somber mood. Wednesday the first arrived and I was on pins and needles all day.

I watched the news for any reports of a car accident, and there was nothing in my area. I had so many questions, was this even real? But I felt like if I couldn't trust the voice that gave me the message then what good is any of this. A few days later Charlene stopped by to return the props she had borrowed. Obviously nothing happened to her. She told me she stayed home all day!

I felt bad in a way, I wished there was some other sign of validation I could get that the message in fact did prevent a tragedy. But for now I think I will just have to accept that it's possible it did.

I discussed the issue with a couple of friends before I made the decision to tell her. One friend said he didn't think he would share it. I realized it was not much different actually, than if you were standing outside on the street and saw a car coming toward your friend, would you just stand there and let it hit her? Or would you yell and say watch out- get out of the way? Even if the car ultimately would have missed her, you might still have wanted to yell just in case.

What if I had not said anything to her and she HAD died in a car crash? I would have to live with that the rest of my life. I think I will take potentially looking silly over not giving a message if it regards life or death.

March 29, 2015 I dreamed I was getting ready to take an in person workshop with Sue Bryce (portrait photographer instructor for beauty portraits). I was already there. I saw Sue and preparations were being made for the class.

July 15 and 16 I took a two day workshop with Sue at the Costa Mesa Canon Experience Center. It was a last minute workshop that was put together only a week or two before the class.

DREAM ABOUT A DREAM

April 6, 2015- *I dreamed I was being told about dreams coming true. There was one from the current journal that would come true today*. September 13 2015, I was talking to my mom on the phone and said hey- I forgot to tell you I had a dream about you in March and it turned out to be about your house flood. And I asked her what date she discovered it. She confirmed April 6th was the day she discovered the leak damage and called her Insurance company. I think this was the first time I had a dream informing me that another dream was going to play out that day or any day for that matter.

I was also using the journal for some other things- I wrote an odd déjà vu experience down today. April 6, I went to the Postal Annex. I parked my car next to an SUV with a golden retriever waiting for his owner to come back. The windows were down halfway, and

I started to flirt with the dog and say hello. While I sat there a car drove by behind us which started a déjà vu with a second car also going by in the opposite direction. Then I noticed the car with the dog said Rodeo on it, and made me think of my brother Phil's golden retriever named Rodeo.

Rodeo died suddenly at home in July. He was only 4 years old. He had died at some point during the day when my brother and his wife were at work. Their remaining golden retriever Tres was sitting next to Rodeo, his buddy. I actually did tell my brother that day that I had a déjà vu experience involving Rodeo, and I will say it did give me a feeling of concern for him. But at the time he was not showing any symptoms that anything could be wrong with him, and the déjà vu experience didn't really spell out anything to be concerned about.... It was just unusual. I had never met my brother's current dogs. They live in Texas and at the time of this event, I hadn't seen them in years.

VISITORS

I had a couple of dreams that I think relate to my niece Annie, my brother Cory's daughter. Annie had been living with her mother and step father for the last year in Los Angeles. I had not seen her since she was about three months old. I had called her last year to invite her to come out with my kids and my brother James' daughter Malone, so she could meet her cousins but she declined.

Prior to last year, she was living with her dad and brother in Texas, but she was not getting along with any of them for various reasons and they were having a lot of drama. I was not told until recently (June 2015), that it was largely because she had friended some boys in the neighborhood who were bullying her brother, and when asked to separate herself from them she refused, so my brother decided to send her to live with her mother. April 10, 2015- I *dreamed about a girl staying in a small building like a guest house out back.* April 18, 2015- *I was at a school open house and was going from room to room. There was a chair with a basket for catching bullies- they were made to sit on the chair.*

May 16, 2015 *I dreamed I saw a girl walking on the sidewalk. She was young, but it was as if I didn't know her. She needed a dress and shoes. I was going to buy a dress and shoes for her. Then she came with me to a dressing room and she was going to try the clothes on.*

May 16, 2015 I attended a book signing with Psychic Medium Thomas John in La Jolla. There were about 20 people in attendance in the small bookstore. I arrived late and there was one seat left in the front row. Thomas saw me come in and motioned for me to sit up front. After he gave his talk about his book **Never Argue with a Dead Person**, he started to do readings randomly for the audience.

After he chatted with a couple of other people he pointed in my direction, and he started naming a lot of names of my dead family members. I was stunned! He said your father in law is here, and James, and then he said "Who is Annie?" I said she is my middle brother's daughter.

He didn't like to deal with connections that were that far removed from the person in attendance, so he brushed it off, plus she was not dead, and so he wasn't going to be speaking with her like he would a dead person. Sitting in the audience at the book store, I witnessed surprising details that came effortlessly to him about family members of strangers sitting in the small group in attendance. And then he pointed at me directly and without blinking an eye he said looking straight at me- "You're writing a book! It's a memoir, and I see you going through old photos and old pages. He continued, "You need to get organized with it, you are going to manifest this, and it will do well, but you need to get organized".

Wow. That was right on the mark! Sifting through 14 dream journals, and a couple of other journals with daily pages and synchronicities has been a daunting task. Not only that, but somehow I have on the earlier reviews ended up missing some very significant events, and while writing all of this I have continued to add more that I have found.

The next day I went to his seminar and the small morning group of 7 I had signed up for, was given another chance at a reading. He told me many things, but again out of the blue he asked "who is Annie?" And again he didn't pursue it. I really didn't know what to think. As far as I knew she was doing just fine with her mom in LA.

The seminar was a full day, and I was just so amazed at the ease he was able to access information that was so personal to the people in attendance. I knew I wanted to reign in whatever I was randomly accessing in my sleep, and learn to make use of it in waking hours so that I might actually be able to help people with it. That's not to take away from what happened frequently when I was asleep, whether it was a mystical experience or a precognitive dream. There is real value there in terms of just seeing a glimpse of what is on other planes of existence, learning to be open to growth opportunities. If there is anything that is at the core of all that I have been trying to learn it is wanting to grow spiritually.

With all of this which has happened this year, the seemingly "random" push that led me to revisit my journals, and a medium telling me to get organized, when I had stacks of journals to go through again, and try to figure out how I was going to sort it all, there has been something in the background helping at different steps on the way. Though I can't see them, I know they are there and little a-ha moments happen and I know I'm headed in the right direction.

There are also some dreams that came true which would provide a good dramatic story, but are too sensitive to the people involved, and even with name changes it just doesn't seem right to share the details beyond a vague summary of dreaming of someone's arrest 15 years before it happened, aspects of my husband's future second wife before he even met her, and of course at the time there was no way to know what these would turn out to be related to, but only upon review and noticing the linking elements that tied them together did it become clear what they were about.

Then, Saturday, May 23rd, I had a strong sense of spirits in my room at night while I was trying to go to sleep. It felt like they were there but trying for me not to see them to avoid startling me. At one point I woke up and saw someone right beside the bed, only two feet away at most! - a kid. I freaked out, and I flapped the sheets and they went right through him, and he vanished! I didn't know who it could have been at first. After some thought I decided it could have been my brother's youngest boy Tommy who had drowned when he was only five years old. Why would he be showing up at my bedside? I had never met him, and he passed away about ten years before. I was going to find out thirteen days later.

On June 5th there was a knock at my front door. I had just gotten home from the dog park with my dogs, and had put them in their gated area in the kitchen.

I first looked through the peep hole as I always do to see if it was a sales person. I have a no soliciting sign on the door and not surprisingly, it doesn't usually stop the sales people. But I wanted to see if I could determine if it was anyone I knew before opening the door.

I saw a man and a teenage girl. I had no idea who it was. So I opened the door just a crack. The man asked me if I was Kim Treffinger. I said yes I am. I looked over at the girl. I recognized her as my niece Annie. I had seen her photos on Facebook.

I said oh, are you guys visiting in town today? The man said "I tried to call and leave a message, did you get it?" I said no, I hadn't gotten any message. He said "do you know who this girl is?" I said yes I did. I had seen her photos online many times from my brother and she and I had communicated last year when I tried to get her to come out with my kids and my niece Malone in LA, but she had declined. Again I said are you guys in town visiting today? I had a feeling I knew where he was going, but I was pretty much in shock.

He said "hold on a second and let me check something in the car". Then he started up the car and drove off! He had dumped her back pack on the sidewalk. Then after he had gone around the corner, he called me on the phone and said "is she safe with you?" I pretty much proceeded to lose it with him and told him what he was doing was probably illegal.

Annie meanwhile had no idea where she was, nobody had told her she was getting left here. But it turned out they had some serious drama between all of them. She had been set to fly back to my brother's in Texas in a few more days. But my brother was going through a divorce with his second wife, and they had sold their house, and he was in a little 2 bedroom apartment with his older son. So for the time being it seemed like we should give it a try for her to live with me. A week later she had her 16th birthday, and since she had arrived with one pair of shoes, and we went clothes shopping.

ZARA

I have developed a new direction in my art in the last two years, and built up a significant collection that I had been trying to figure out how to get it out there in the world. It was developed in a time of intense grief, and the particular process that I employed on the images and the choice of subject matter spoke to me as being very real relief from my grief after a convergence of losing my amazing cat PJ and a relationship, and broken foot. I was very broken.

While contemplating the scope of this project, it dawned on me that I might like to create a card deck to accompany the book. Suddenly in a frenzy of a day and a half I had selected images, created content and laid out almost all of the 50 cards. It all came together almost effortlessly. I had all the images I needed already, not only for the card deck, but for the book cover itself. I couldn't believe it.

I went to bed one night a few days after this all came together and asked to meet one of my guides. I got a picture of a beautiful black woman, inside a card with amazing and beautiful designs surrounding her. She told me her name was Zara. I believe she is South African.

First of all, I wasn't expecting a guide for creating my card deck. That was a total surprise, and I was both amused and delighted with the image. I saw the image of the woman on the card, and I heard a woman's voice say Szara. I asked her is it Sara? And then I was presented with her named spelled in front of me on the card Zara.

I have found when you can get to a place of asking questions within the dream or experience you are more likely to get more information. Up until now most information of this nature tends to be very minimal beyond the visual image itself. This may just be how I best process information or remember it so I can write it down, and others may have a very different experience.

SPIRIT SENDS ME LOOKING

March 23, 2015 I dreamed about a boy named Cameron who was a high school friend of the daughter of a client of mine that I had photographed several years ago. Cameron and the girl had been at a bon fire party with high school friends. Someone threw gasoline on the fire and it flew up into the girl's face and Cameron rushed to block the fire from getting on her and he took the brunt of it and was burned over 90% of his body.

I followed some of the tragedy on Facebook with my clients posting the hospital status of both kids along with prayer requests.

I saw that Cameron was put into a coma because the pain was too intense. Infections set in, and after a couple of months of trying everything to save him, he passed away. This dream came the day after I learned of his passing.

I dreamed I may have already dreamed about Cameron asking me to give a message to his friends and family. I saw an old notebook with an entry about it (but I didn't think there was anything to this). Then I heard him telling me something but it was too fast to keep up. He said tell everyone I love them. I'm sorry this happened, and something about Ryan, and someone could have his papers and his phone. I wrote in my journal asking for help with this because I didn't feel it was enough information to feel secure in giving this message to his family. I asked for something I wouldn't know from Facebook and I got a little dog named Jordy. Then March 24- *I dreamed I was being told to look in the dream books again for Cameron and the fire pit accident. I was told that things had been set up very specifically so I could help others.* But I wasn't told which journal to look in. There are 14 journals and over 2000 pages! *I saw a woman dressed in blue who seemed to have done the work and it seemed that it wasn't easy.*

Then I saw an orange Peugeot like my Papa had (only my Papa's was white). I hadn't seen one in a long time but it looked brand new. I was in a parking lot with a man and his van and he was trying to help me.

.I went through all 14 journals looking for anything remotely close to this story of Cameron. I had had THREE dreams telling me it was in my old journals. But I found nothing of Cameron. I was frustrated! I felt like my dreams were lying to me. I had never experienced this before. I reached out for help from James Van Praagh, and I wrote him an email. He told me that I needed to get grounded and keep trying. I need to meditate more.

I did however find several other dreams I had somehow missed previously. As I read through the pages this time, I started to see something I had not noticed before, and that was how things can overlap,

and I can be other people than myself even though in the dream I think it's me. So while I was on a wild goose chase for anything on Cameron, I found little gems I had completely missed before. In some ways it was a big lesson for me, so that now going forward as I continue to keep my journals, I might be better at picking out the ones that are more likely to happen, and as I write this, I know I have a handful of dreams that are primed to happen in some form or other between now and next year

I know my mother would have liked a warning about her home getting flood damage from a broken pipe, and I would have liked to have helped out with that, but there wasn't enough information in that first dream for me to understand it at the time. Now, after seeing how I should have interpreted the dream, I would say there was an issue with plumbing and pipes with her drain being wide open. But there was no water that I saw in the dream. Maybe it wouldn't have been visible yet in March, but the furniture was all out of her house, so that point doesn't seem like much. She ended up being in a hotel for three months while the insurance company muddled through getting the repairs done for her.

And while she was in the hotel she fell over a carpet replacement job in the hallway, injured herself and is now on physical therapy to boot. A dream about a little caution sign around new carpeting might have been helpful.

I realize I have done quite a bit of complaining about the ways that the dreams have not helped me, and yet, I cannot stress enough the value just in showing these connections, because I do believe it can happen for anyone. And sometimes dreams do come through with a clear message.

DREAMING FOR OTHERS

March 24, 2015 *I dreamed I was with a small group of people. We were going to go biking together. My bike was the same teal color as my road bike, but the body frame looked more futuristic and modern and it was mentioned how they liked how it looked. It needed to be tested before going on a ride. I got on and was trying to see how it rode. One guy thought it needed something extra done to it, but I thought it might work anyway. It had a long trail of a strip of fabric stuck to it and the gears might have needed adjusting. We were going to ride to a place to eat.*

My friend Rachel had been talking about getting a new bike to ride with some friends. The bike was a gift to her in July, I don't believe she had any input on the color or style, and it was teal and futuristic looking. She did ride with a small group to go get a bite to eat in July.

Now in the dream, I was the woman with the bike. It feels like more frequently I am dreaming for others and the person who I think is me is actually someone else. Going forward that will be something I will have to try to grapple with. Is the dream for ME or someone else? And how will I tell the difference?

In this case, I was aware that a new bike was in the plans for Rachel, but I had no active role in the bike acquisition or recommendation whatsoever, and she didn't have much say either. I realize this switch may have been more prevalent in my dreams than I had realized.

This is a definite turning point for me. I feel a strong sense of having been helped invisibly with many of these, maybe by the guide named Debbie dressed in blue, and even with timing of things that happen in my life whether I have dreamed about them or not. I have a heightened sense of synchronicity and serendipity. I recognize the familiar PINGS of things coming together when multiple people are saying the same peculiar things to me. I feel like I'm on a very special train at times and I can't wait to see what's at the next stop when the doors open.

WHAT GOES IN MUST COME OUT

In terms of spiritual growth in regard to dreams, one of the things that sunk in deeply for me was the vast amount of dreams I recorded especially in the earlier years, which were simply processing my sense of lack of power in my life, lack of accomplishment up until then, and to make up for it I had countless fanciful dreams of romantic encounters with movie stars and idealized male figures. Reviewing all of them nearly 20 years later was extremely humbling. I clearly do not want to have any more shallow dreams of romance with movie stars. I'm never going to marry Kevin Costner! So please can we stop with those already? My gosh. It was embarrassing even to me.

What stands out from all of that are a few things. Number one, it was clear I did not have enough going on for myself in the way of personal or professional development, and number two I was "over feeding" myself on entertainment. And it took over my dream life as well.

The good news is that when you learn how important it is to know that when you feed yourself food and substance in your daily life that is healthy for you, which sustains you and makes room for you to grow and flourish, that the fluff that makes no difference at all starts to wash away.

That is not to say that I am yet to achieve a perfectly clean slate in my dream life, and that I have a perfect understanding of all of this. Far from it, but I see a connection, and I know that when I shut off the *noise* in my life, it allows room for spirit to come in and support me, which in turn, allows me to support others as well.

All of this is really like a big bowl of soup in a way. It's messy at times, murky or clear. Trying to make your way through it can be a challenge. There is usually something good there. Outside of that, there are also times where it is utterly mind blowing whether it's a lucid dream, or visiting with a master teacher or hugging and kissing a dearly departed loved one as if you were really with them.

There is so much out there, that I think I have only scratched the surface. Whether you have a dream that happens the very same day, or one that doesn't happen for decades later, writing them down in a thoughtful descriptive way, that includes as much detail as you can possibly remember will eventually, I believe, result in some psychic activity for the dreamer.

JOURNAL REVIEW

Coming up with a review plan is a good idea. I created a separate binder for the dreams that were "hits". I copied them and keep them there. I know many people these days would recommend a program or app to record your dreams, or even to voice record them. I say whatever works best for you is ok. For me personally, there is something extra in seeing my handwriting on the page with the dream. It's an easier space to draw an image, if that seems important to the dream.

I feel there is a stronger spiritual connection to handwriting than there is to typing something into software. It's more unique to you than standardized font symbols that would be used in typing, and I like to believe that a part of the energy of the dream is imbedded into the paper when you write it by hand. This does make it harder to track things, but I guess

I am old school that way.

Even if I typed dream recall into a computer which allowed me to keyword search something, I'm not sure searching that way would accomplish much, you would already have to have a sense of something specific you were looking for. But if your handwriting is not legible, then you may as well type. I think recording by voice will make it more difficult to search anything later, and take longer, but if you find yourself with no other means at the moment, then certainly use a voice recorder and maybe one that can do voice to text for you. There are many voice recording apps available for your phone. But then be sure to write or type it out later.

Dreams are not usually literal. You will many times have to analyze them and see how something is representing something else. For instance, in one dream I saw stilts for walking on, and we stepped up onto them and used them for walking. But the description itself was a closer match to the actual event, and my term stilts would be irrelevant. It was referencing a "walking stick" used on a hike… the description was there- used for walking, but the image was not quite right which made it harder to decipher.

When I saw 3 linking elements: my daughter being carried on someone's back, Disneyland, and the "sticks for walking" it came together for me. You have to be a detective, and though I've read this dream many times, (it was in my first journal) but the event itself did not occur for nearly 9 years.

I would recommend monthly reviews of journals if you want to get serious about this, and yearly for ALL of your journals. This means you should take care in the type of journals that you invest in, that they will hold up over time. While a spiral bound book might be easy, it's going to get worn out with frequent reviews. A couple of mine are barely holding together.

But again I would recommend copying out anything that comes up as a "hit" and keeping it in a separate binder for your collection.

When I find dreams or events that were a hit or something unusual to remember, I tab the pages with sticky page flags and write a label of what it was. I note the date the event happened if I can remember it. My books all have dozens of flags on them now.

At first I would review them weekly, then monthly, and then unfortunately I only randomly reviewed from time to time, thinking nothing much was going on in most cases. Unless something happened within the week or two weeks following a dream, I generally completely forgot my dreams, until I looked back and remembered it again, and realize that it may take you some time to learn how to decipher them.

When you start to ask the question who am I in this dream? Is it me or someone I know or will know? I think it's easier to put ourselves into the shoes (literally) of someone we already know. But I suppose it depends on the situation of the dream. Anything is possible. Especially up there.

WHEN YOU CAN'T REMEMBER A DREAM

When I was having trouble remembering my dreams in the morning, I had a separate journal for my morning pages. I was following Julia Cameron's *Artist's Way* book, and that was a tool to help you find your artist path. What I discovered was that it was also extremely helpful for a number of other things as well. The goal is to write non-stop three consecutive pages of whatever comes into your mind. Don't judge it, just write free flow.

It can be junk thoughts or what is going on in your home at the time, concerns you might have, planning out your day, what you are grateful for, anything at all. It's like a brain dump. Dumping out stuff to make room for more. Making this room for more creates space for your creative mind and your memory to work together.

Try it for a week at least, and see if it makes a difference. I found that when I unlocked the block to remembering my dreams, they came rapidly and over a period of time they developed, became more detailed and vivid. At the peak I was writing as many as ten pages of dreams a day. That's a lot for a mom with two little kids. Looking back on it now, it's kind of a miracle I persisted even when the kids were bickering and calling for me to get up, or joining me on the bed and using my knees to climb on like a jungle gym while I feverishly wrote the dreams before they might evaporate like a bubble bursting.

There is also a benefit to going through with doing the motions as if you had remembered your dream. I think there is something here to programming yourself, and communicating to your higher self or dream self that you are serious about wanting to engage with your dream life. And we get back what we put into it.

We survived, everyone got breakfast and off to school. If you are reading this book, I will assume you have more than a passing interest in your dreams and are curious about being more serious and engaged with them. If you have young children at home who are too much of a distraction in the morning, try setting your alarm clock 15-20 min. before your kids might waken. I know this is a sleep sacrifice, but if you do this regularly it will reset your sleep pattern and should readjust your dream time as well, so that you can wake undisturbed and get your dreams recorded.

What I learned is that dreams WANT to be remembered. We sleep the equivalent of a 56 hour work week every week or 100 days a year. A good chunk of that time is dreaming. We can use and access that part of our life. There are very interesting things to be accessed.

Whether it comes from our own higher self, guides, teachers or God, it is always there waiting for us to take an interest and engage with it, see what kind of adventure we can make of it, and what it will encourage us to do in the way of bettering ourselves in our waking lives.

Even the dreams that are not precognitive have lessons for us. They can be humbling at times when they reflect difficulties we may be having. When we review and begin to see patterns, it allows for deeper contemplation about where our attention is in our lives as they mirror back to us a myriad of possibilities, and can give us a chance to make some different choices if we feel that will be beneficial for us to grow.

Many of my dreams in the early years of my recording them revolved around shopping and celebrities, and which celebrity I had a crush on at the time. I see now I was avoiding deeper issues. Spending too much time floating around in the "fluff", and not enough substance.

Sure, a fun dream can be exhilarating and take us away from stresses that we may be feeling, and there is nothing wrong with that, but when you see a pattern of them over and over and over again... it's a sign that something is out of balance.

There are many books out there on what your dreams mean, if you dream of water it relates to emotions and that kind of thing. That is not what I have wanted to focus on for this book. Maybe at some later date I will contemplate more on that. I have tried mainly to determine whether a dream had precognitive or spiritual connections or not. There are many who believe that every single element in a dream is you the dreamer. When it comes to precognitive dreams, I have to say I don't believe that to be true. And in fact many times I, the dreamer, have turned out to be somebody else.

ASK AND IT IS GIVEN

For years I mostly allowed the dreams to just come, and they did. And I gradually grew frustrated with the randomness. I wanted a sense of control. I have had success with going to bed at night and asking a question of something I would like information on that would be helpful for my life, for a friend or a project I was working on. Many times I will get some sort of response. It has not always been what I wanted, or enough information, but more times than not there is a response that is related to the question.

How to improve the clarity is something that I continue to deal with, but I know when certain conditions are in place, I experience a sense of progress in how dreams are coming, and even events in my waking life coming together in "unexpected" ways.

To set a tone for a good night sleep and create an open space for questions to be answered or experience something at a level that you have not yet experienced before, I would recommend planning a day loosely with the intention in mind to do major activities earlier in the day if any are planned. Possibly meditate in the morning before going out.

If you are new to meditation you may want to find some peaceful music to have playing quietly. There are many guided meditation audio recordings or even just instrumental music that you may find relaxing. Limit exterior stimulations, find a quiet space where you will not be disturbed for at least ten minutes.

If you are more experienced with meditation, by all means try for 20-45 minutes. Avoid alcohol or drugs which will lower your vibration. Clear your mind, breathe and allow for the image of breathing in a white light and taking it into your heart space, and breathe it out letting go of what is not needed.

Meditation is a practice where there are many ways to practice it, and finding one method that works best for you would be most beneficial.

Walking in nature and yoga are a couple of other examples of kinds of meditation. I encourage people to seek out a variety and see the difference for themselves. The energy in group meditation is also a powerful experience. So a good meditation in the morning to start the day, then at night about an hour before you go to bed, try a meditation again for 10-30 minutes. Allow for your last hour before bed to be quiet.

Avoid dramatic media right before bed, television, movies, etc. Make a peaceful space. You may want to play soft meditation music, have a candle lit with an intention to bring clarity, or abundance or love. Whatever you are wanting to develop in your life.

At bedtime (blow the candle out), say a prayer of protection, so that as you open yourself up to the cosmic energy of the universe, you are protecting yourself from lower energies that are not in your best interest.

Consider all that you have to be thankful for you in your life, no matter how small. Allow the gratitude to surround you, be at peace with it as if it was a living energy. Let this feeling resonate with you for a few minutes, feel it deeply, give it space to live with you.

Then make a strong mental intention that you are looking for information or guidance from only the highest good for all, from the light of God. Repeat this to yourself as you fall asleep. You may also repeat, and even write it out on a piece of paper, what you are wishing to know more about from your dream time.

Have a notebook by the bed at all times with a

pen. You may awaken in the middle of the night with an experience or dream. I recommend writing it down immediately and take no chance of it evaporating in the morning. This way you will also have more detail than if you wait until morning.

Saying a prayer:

You may have some prayers that speak to you. I recommend looking for a prayer to use at bedtime when preparing to open up to higher source. I have not often felt like I needed it, but I think the process of doing it does enhance the experience, sets your intention, and provides another level of security. The prayer provided below is from the Unity Church. An all- inclusive non-denominational organization.

PRAYER OF PROTECTION:

The light of God surrounds me: The love of God enfolds me; The power of God protects me; The presence of God watches over me. Wherever I am, God is!

In my dream history, the time of night a dream or event occurred seemed to play a role in the type of dream or event. If I went to bed between 10 and 11pm for example, from 11:30pm until 3 am, anything that occurred was more likely to be a spiritual nature. My personal belief, and I have heard this elsewhere is that between midnight and 3am, there are enough people sleeping in your area, that the quietness makes room for spirit to come through.

I don't know how this would impact locations like Las Vegas where they never sleep. I have always been in places where things do slow down very much during those hours of the night (or morning so to speak). Dreams that happened just before waking in the morning were generally about daily life. So when I woke to see something floating in the room, or I "dreamed" of my guides or teachers, they were always before 3am.

So I would say, if you want to meet your guides, and you wake before 3 am, and have a chance to go back to sleep- repeat to yourself:

I want to meet my guide as you fall back to sleep. I have asked to meet one and the same night got a result. But there were many many times I asked and did not think I got a response. So if it doesn't happen right away, don't assume that it never will, it may just take some time.

Keep in mind that there is much more than we may ever know to this, and we have work to accomplish in our waking time as well, that impacts what we receive in our sleep. Be careful to avoid negative thinking where possible. We are most open for these experiences when we keep a light frame of mind and allow good energy to flow through us.

Guides will come in their own time, usually when you least expect it, but it is usually going to coincide with something else going on in your life- whether you have decided to take a class, or you are having some kind of turning point in your life. It usually will come as a reinforcement that you are on the right track with your spiritual growth. That is the goal they seek for us, and we are given little signs to let us know that we are moving in the right direction.

Guides may show you some ways in which they are helping you, some of it may make sense and some of it may not. They also may change from time to time, so it can be good to try to "check in" and see who is helping you if you feel you have reached a new level of understanding in your life. They really do have our highest good at heart, and take their job very seriously. In fact, most of mine have always been in business clothes, to indicate they are working for me. That could be a message that is personal to me, that I would respond to and respect, and possibly whatever would reach you the best is what you might experience.

When I have seen my Papa in dreams over the years since his death in 1990, he has evolved over that time, and now when I see him, he looks dashing in a suit and tie. He drove a fork lift for Dupont most of his life and was a coal miner as a young man. He quit school in 6th grade to work and help support his large family of brothers. He seemed comfortable in casual clothes most of his life. I had only seen him wear a suit once in my whole life, and that was at my wedding.

I take the "message" of seeing him in a suit as a sign of his advancement of some kind. It doesn't necessarily mean he loves to dress that way, but it's a symbol that he is working on things in a new way and taking things more seriously than maybe he did before. It's a non-verbal way to communicate something- what they are wearing. Change or growth in this case.

TWO BODIES

Can you imagine opening a book you had written of dreams from 17 years ago to find multiple dreams that came true and you never knew it before, AND to watch one of them unfold right before your eyes with a witness, which you dreamed all the way back then?

The journey the journal itself had taken from shelf to shelf in the house over the years, in a stack with the others, then boxed up in the garage for years. It was utterly mind blowing. It was practically like experiencing a ripple or tear in the time continuum.

For me, this journey has given me more questions than answers, but it certainly has answered a few things for me. Number one is that we are not taught the true nature of reality. There is so much to learn and I don't think any one source on earth today has all the answers, but more and more, some of these things are being tested by science.

We have two bodies. We don't grow up with that notion at all. But we do. Some cultures are more knowledgeable about this than others. But Western culture for the most part seems to have a blind eye to it.

Our physical body that we are born with, and grow old in if we are lucky, houses and is a shell for our energy body. Our energy body is ageless, timeless and has possibly experienced many other lifetimes in a different physical body prior to this one, and after this one passes away, at some point in the future, may choose to have a new body and a new life, quietly carrying with it previous experiences and knowledge.

The energy body can travel. It can travel when sleeping or meditating. The energy body maintains a connection to the physical body so that at a split microsecond it can again be fully present in the physical body if needed (until we die). But where does it go? Where CAN it go? These are great questions since the beginning of man.

I imagine I will be trying to work these out until my own last breaths one day. From reading other accounts of life after death, near death and out of body experiences, it seems that reality is more fluid than we know. There are many layers and levels and endless places to go, endless kinds of other beings to encounter, and other worlds I would imagine.

But I have only experienced dreams with the approximation of planet Earth and I guess what many people might call Heaven. But at the time is was more like a school, or a white place. I think I will be sorting out the people I encountered along the way for some time. Unless I wake up one of these days and "they" suddenly decide to share the secrets with me.

There is so much more to learn about theories of our energy body. I am still learning about it myself, and I would encourage anyone with an interest to do some research and read the work that others have done. I will put a list of suggested reading at the end, as a recommended starting point. This is a life-long endeavor to learn about energy.

CHILDREN REMEMBER

Little children are more aware of where they have just come from. Until the age of about 4 or 5 and they acclimate into the rules of the life they have chosen to grow up in. As toddlers they are still sometimes aware of the cosmic or heavenly place they have just come from, and often times can remember the previous lifetime they lived.

There are many many cases of these memories that children have told, and some which have even been documented where the child remembered a critical identifying piece of information about the person they had previously lived as, and they actually found, and met surviving family members of their previous family.

When my middle brother Cory was less than two years old, out of the blue one day he told us "I know what it's like to be in a coffin. I was a cowboy, and I died in a rodeo". We could not believe what he said. It was completely unrelated to anything we had experienced. Not only that, but it was complete sentences with words that made sense. How did he ever hear the word coffin before that day? Or rodeo? Our family was not into that kind of culture.

Children may be encouraged to share their dreams if they remember them. When they are old enough to draw a picture with pencil or crayons, they might be able to draw a picture of the dream if they remember it. When they are 7-9 they may be ready to begin keeping their first dream journal. Family members might enjoy sharing their dreams with each other.

I believe if we start to take dreams more seriously and teach children to pay attention to them, they may learn to access information for themselves as well, and by the time they are adults, could have an interesting grasp of their dreaming life.

LOCATION LOCATION LOCATION!

When we travel in our waking life, we may find ourselves at a location that we are excited to be at for one reason or another, or that location may have a strong spiritual connection that continues to thrive in that area. You might call it a HOT SPOT or a VORTEX. Some locations may be more spiritually centered like Sedona or surrounding areas to that location, or places where old history is kept alive with vintage homes, memorials, old buildings. And certainly near areas where there was heavy war activity or atrocities. Some areas may be a combination of both. The spirit world is never one or the other alone.

Many people have said they have experienced angels, and while I don't necessarily doubt in their existence, I personally have never encountered one YET, that I was aware of. I would hope that an encounter with a being such as an angel would be memorable. So I am inclined to think it hasn't happened.

Having gone through this process there has been a learning curve, and I feel that will continue. Just when you think you start to get something figured out, a surprise sneaks up like the revelation that I have been other people in dreams many times, and now that I am just feeling like I am getting a handle on trying to tell which ones might come true.

Now I have to take another look at the dreams that seemed to be regarding ME, and ask myself if it's really about me, or is it someone else? I would really like to have more clarity on this matter. I know it will play out at some point one way or the other. Does it take away the surprise element if I know too much? I have thought about this one many times. While it's nice to be able to help people, and that is my goal at some point, for myself, I suppose it would take away some of life's surprise that I think we take for granted.

I think of the years that I had stopped keeping my dream journals after 2002. What might I have missed? Thirteen years' worth of dreams and experiences unrecorded. This could have been a very different book. But it would have been a mountain of material to review, and seeing how I have had to review the content I do have multiple times, it could have taken years to sort it all out. I am going to trust that all is well from the way I was pushed to pull the journals out of boxes and review them again. Something like that could have happened sooner I suppose, and it didn't.

Keeping track of our dreams has not become mainstream. And this may be but another little pebble in the stream of life, but it is one more voice for people to hear. At some point there may be a tipping point, and the tide will turn and parents will teach their children more about the nature of reality with spirit and energy and dreams. Dreams will be more valued, because you never know what you are up to when you are asleep. You won't know if you don't write it down.

TELLING IT LIKE IT IS

When you are preparing to write it down, it might be helpful to consider describing it as if you are describing a movie or a television show. But in as much detail as you can manage to grab from it.

Some things to consider are:

What role did you play? Is it possible you were in the place of someone else?

Were you able to see yourself in the dream, or were you a participant where you were not aware of your appearance?

Did you have any idea of the time frame of the dream? Is it current time? Past or Present?

What odd things stand out?

Did you dream in color or black and white? What colors were there?

What did people say? Who was there? How did you feel?

Initially you may only recall a sentence or two worth of a dream. It's ok. Write it down anyway. The more you do this, gradually you will remember more and more, and if you persist, one day the floodgates will open and you will have more dreams to write down than you have time for.

It is also important to not judge your description of a dream at first. What I mean is don't be so quick to edit your words. Just let them come. If you feel there is another way to say it, write that down too, but trust that the first way you want to describe a dream will have some relevance and meaning, even if it doesn't seem like it at first.

A few of my friends have started sharing their dreams with me, asking me to help them sort it out. So far, it has been fun to see that they were experiencing a similar thing to me in that their visual idea of the dream was not matching the verbal description the same way. The verbal description had more clues than they expected by their choice of words. And you could see a light bulb go on when they realized that. So read your description back to yourself as if you were telling it to someone else. Does anything stand out to you as something that might have two meanings? Both the visual and the description will have meaning, even if the visual turns out to be off later.

Just as I described the stilts, having no idea I was writing the functionality of a walking stick. But then finding the dream with the relevant elements years later, it tied together and I could see my verbal description was more relevant to the event that played out than my visual picture was in terms of how it played out, but the image of the stilts portrayed a performance, balancing act, and playful spirit which were also relevant to the real situation.

A friend described walking with a group of four people. One of them was "ahead" of the rest of them. In her mind it was simply the position of the people on the sidewalk, but to me it stood out as placing this person first, and the dream was likely about him. Be on the lookout for words like this.

Recently as I have begun to talk more about what I am writing, and that I am starting to see myself as someone who will help even in a small way to get people to think more about their dreaming life, I cannot help but notice a large disinterest in dreams as anything to spend valuable time with. In a way it seems that most people are literally sleep walking through life, just trying to get the day to day activities and requirements taken care of. I realize that is no small task.

But I imagine a world where children are encouraged to remember their dreams, to talk about them, write them down or draw their dreams and keep them in a safe place for contemplation at a later date.

I feel if we start out learning to value our dreams as children, the opportunity for development of engagement is huge. The opportunity to learn to connect with our spirit self and guides from an early age is enormous. Learning to take control of your dreams from childhood could likely have great impact on confidence, creativity, and expression among other things. A different world view would emerge for people as they connect with the concept that time is a very interesting thing.

If we learned to engage with our dreams as children, we would learn how to ask for information, and guidance, and also how to control dreams and have less nightmares as a result.

The dream world is our natural connection to spirit, every single night. It waits for us to care about engaging with it. If we show it no care, it will likely not perform for us. If however, we take great interest and invest some thought and commit to recording our dreams, great things are possible. Each dreamer has their own path, their own growth to journey with.

Give it some of your time and it will evolve for you right before your eyes.

People like to give themselves permission to dismiss their dreams: "I never remember my dreams"... and they furrow their eyebrows and scrunch their face up, as if to say- it's a waste of my time, it will never work for me... But that is NOT the case!

I am not one of those who will say I am special because I can have psychic dreams. I happen to believe this can happen for everyone if they give permission and allow themselves to be open to it. I believe this is a natural activity. We just need to have an open mind, because we have not been taught to accept this as a culture. Silly dreams... that's what people like to chalk it up to. Sure there are silly dreams, but there are also dreams that tell of a time decades in the future as well. There are dreams with passed on loved ones, guides, and even God. If people can't find the value in that, I don't know what to say.

Thank you for joining me on this reflection of my journey, and insights I have gained from my own review process. I look forward to engaging with readers.

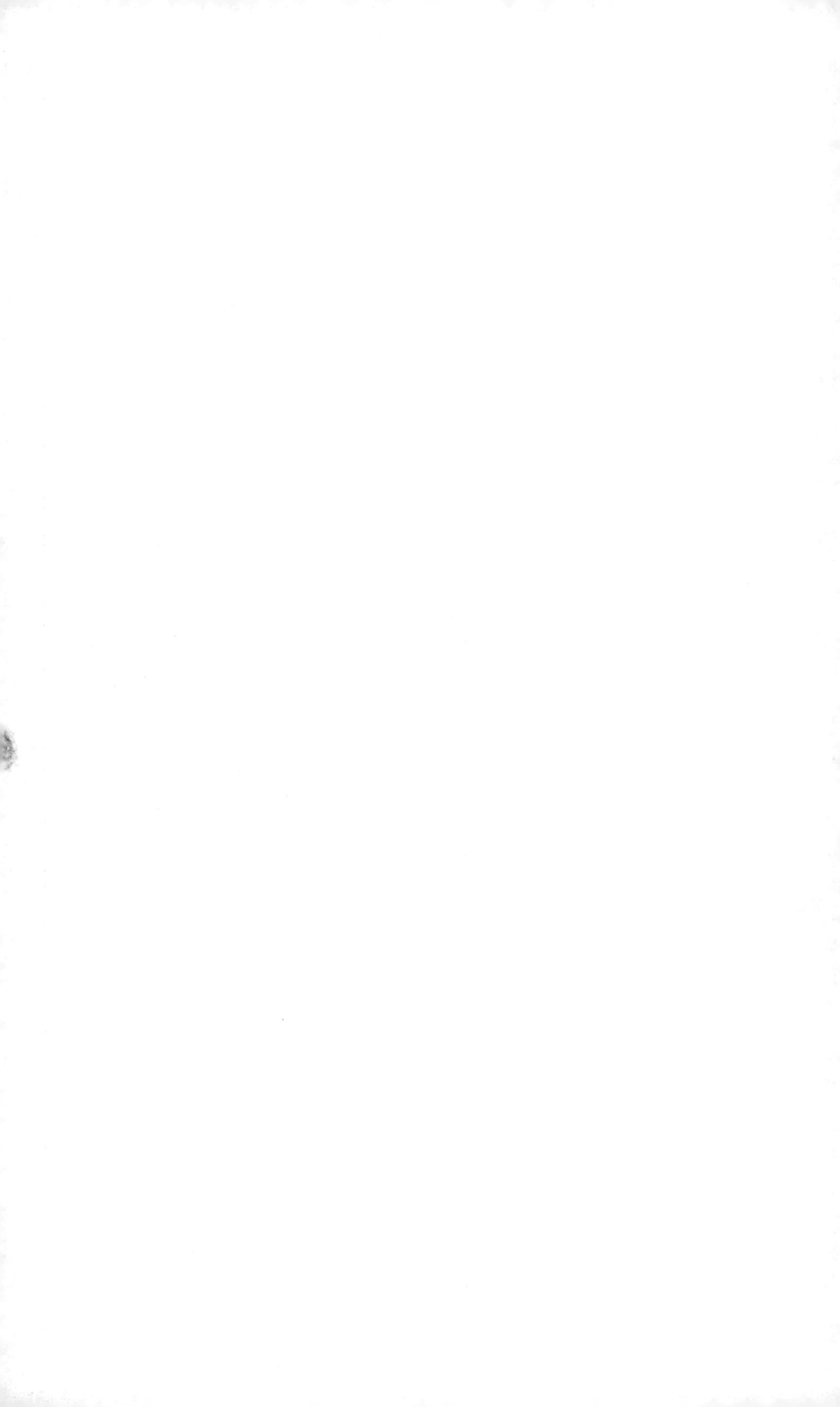

INSPIRATION AND POETRY

Dreams are a fantastic source of inspiration. Sometimes I am amazed by the creativity that comes out in my dreams, and things I never would have thought of in my waking life, come to life in a dream just like a big budget movie. If you are a creative person, this can be a goldmine for you.

In one dream I remember I was visiting a pastel artist friend of mine whom I hadn't seen in years. She was sitting on the ground, legs crossed, and covering herself in colored chalk. It was all over her face and in her hair and on her clothing. Vibrant colors. And if I wasn't surprised enough by that, she took a piece of blue chalk and started to color on her teeth with it while looking me square in the eye, so that all of her teeth were blue. I thought, wow. If I ever write a creative story, this would be an interesting eccentric character.

Whatever it may be, you may dream of doing something you have always wanted to do, and maybe lacked confidence, but a dream showed you that you could do it after all. Or you may envision the kind of home you want to live in. The possibilities are literally endless. The more you desire to engage with your dream life, the more it will engage with you.

There is as much adventure waiting for you, as you are open to receive. Your adventure will be unique to you, and a life long journey will take root, if you make room for it.

I look forward to the evolution of my own dream life, it has made big changes since I started taking notice of it, and then again when I put out requests for meaningful content. These days I don't have the pages and pages of dreams that I had during the "awakening stage", but I have a much higher percentage of dreams that are likely to be relevant to future events.

Currently I am waiting to see how one dream about a future "new relationship" pans out, whether it is about me or a friend, only time will tell. And a possible great adventure is waiting for a missing link to set it in motion. I would love to share it here, but I don't want to taint it. But rest assured that if it comes to pass it will be all over my blog.

The other day I dreamed I heard a man's voice say "I am coming". So I have a sense that something is on the horizon. But I don't have the answer to it yet.

My greatest wish from sharing all of this is to spark people to seek for themselves their own dream journey and find their spiritual connection in dreams and meditation. When you finally realize that the dream world is really a portal to possibilities and alternate realities, and very real past present and future, you will see the world with new eyes, and a new life will unfold for you. The whole world will suddenly be a different place than you thought it was.

You will start to notice a new flow in YOUR world. Synchronicities will arise with perfect timing and more questions with them.

Be open to the possibilities. And take time for gratitude. Gratitude fuels our options.

I still struggle when I see things going on in the world that are not based in peace and love. War and killing of people and animals are really tough things to watch. I don't have the answer to these things. But I know that when we give respect to people and other life forms, we are going in the right direction.

Respect all beings.

Namaste.

One of the most poetic dreams I recorded, and for some inexplicable reasons has made me extremely emotional multiple times. I just cannot put my finger on why I am having this reaction to it, but I think it's a beautiful scene so I'll share it here as a final dream to take flight with...

June 15, 1994

I dreamed I was on a walk with a woman alongside a road, and we came upon my slippers sitting there on the ground. They were both filled with leaves and I picked them up. The woman with me was sure they would have bugs in them, and was acting frightened that I might touch one. I had no such worries and I pulled the leaves out and saw two beautiful butterflies in the bottom. As we were walking up a hill with beautiful houses on the side of the road, the butterflies sat together on my finger and they squeezed it tight with their legs, and I tried to let them fly away, but they kept holding on. I said "go on girls, fly away" and they did.

READING LIST

These are a few suggested titles. This list is far from complete, but there is much good information in the books I have listed. There are many many more, and I hope you will do some serious investigation of your own.

The End of Materialism by Charles Tart

On Life After Death, by Elisabeth Kubler-Ross

The Opening of The Wisdom-Eye H.H. the Dalai Lama Tenzin Gyatso

Realities of the Dreaming Mind, by Swami Sivananda Radha

What Your Dreams Can Teach You, by Alex Lukeman

Explore the World of Lucid Dreaming, by Stephen La Berge Ph.D. & Howard Rheingold

The Intuitive Edge, by Philip Goldberg

Control Your Dreams, by Jayne Gackenbach & Jane Bosveld

Coming Back A Psychiatrist Explores Past Life Journeys by Raymond Moody M.D.

Seth Dreams and Projections of Consciousness, by Jane Roberts

Coming Back; A Psychiatrist Explores Past-Life Journeys, by Raymond A. Moody, Jr.,M.D.

ABOUT THE AUTHOR

For more information about the author and to purchase coaching, or artwork, visit the websites below.

Books, Blog, and Dream Journey Coaching:

www.kimtreffinger.net

Artwork:

www.kimtreffinger.com

Connect-

Instagram: @kimtreff

Twitter: @kimtreffinger

Made in the USA
San Bernardino, CA
14 April 2016